The Power of Being Different

A Success Formula

By

John Paul Carinci

Edited by Donald MacLaren

authorHOUSE™

1663 LIBERTY DRIVE, SUITE 200
BLOOMINGTON, INDIANA 47403
(800) 839-8640
WWW.AUTHORHOUSE.COM

First published by AuthorHouse 05/24/05

ISBN: 1-4208-4698-1 (sc)

Printed in the United States of America
Bloomington, Indiana

This book is printed on acid-free paper.

Dedication

To my father - one of the greatest inspirations in my life, the person I strive to emulate. He was what we all should be - loving and unselfish to the very end.

To my mother – who taught me that I was capable of much more than an average effort.

To my wife, Vera – the love of my life, who tamed a wild bull.

Table of Contents

Nothing in the world can take the place of persistence. Talent will not; nothing is more common than unsuccessful men with talent. Genius will not; unrewarded genius is almost a proverb. Education will not; the world is full of educated derelicts. Persistence and determination alone are omnipotent.

> *--Calvin Coolidge*
> *30th President of the United States*
> *(1923-1929)*

1
Uniqueness Leads To Great Success

Some men see things as they are and say 'why?'
I dream things that never were, and say, 'why not?'

> *--George Bernard Shaw*
> *English Dramatist*
> *(1856-1950)*

Time Moves Faster Than Us

The older one gets, the faster time seems to move. It is my observation that life goes by too fast. Most young people feel it is taking an eternity to become 18 and then 21, so strong is the urge to be considered an adult man or woman. The young man of 21 will soon discover that time seems to move at a faster speed than he realized when he becomes a 35-year-old man. That childhood urge to speed up time will now change into a wish to slow it down when the man reaches 45 and 50. Where are you in your life's journey? Is time speeding up or slowing down for you? At what stage are you?

Do your days seem crammed full of obligations, tasks, deadlines, with a lot less spare time? Are there days when you are so stressed that you would like to drop out of society? Dropping out of society, and disappearing from all the stresses is basically a fantasy, one we all experience at one time or another.

You cannot control the speed of time, but you can control what you accomplish within your limited time. The proper use of work in a time period creates greater success.

Turning A Small Amount of Time Into A Lot of Time

To accomplish more of your personal goals, whether writing, reading, painting, participating in sports, or exercising, you can start by thinking of giving yourself more time in small amounts and forgetting about trying to give the world all your time.

Consider the importance of a 15-minute block of time a day to do something meaningful for yourself. Those "extra" 15 minutes a day would amount to 105 minutes, or 1 3/4 hours a week. If you continue squeezing out those 15 minutes a day, they would equal more than 7 hours a month and more than 91 hours a year. What could you accomplish with your "extra" 91 hours per year?

You could have jogged approximately 350 miles in that year, read approximately 10 new books, or taken a course. You could have prepared for an entirely new field of work or a great new hobby.

It's a lot easier than you think to capture these valuable 15 minutes a day. How you use your time determines what you accomplish in life.

If you allow eight hours sleeping, you are left with 16 hours for working and thinking. And of these 16 hours, you have to allow time for travel, eating, and socializing.

If budgeted properly, you can squeeze out that extra 15 minutes a day that you can call "your time."

Suppose you have been given a $10,000.00 fee as a "time consultant" whose job it is to find those extra 15 minutes every day that can be your time. For the $10,000.00, you can start to write down the wasted minutes. Where are the wasted minutes every day?

Here are some ideas: Can you take a more direct route to work that would give you extra time? Can you take 15 minutes less for lunch? Can you get up 15 minutes earlier to accomplish something? Can you have a lighter dinner that would free up those 15 extra minutes at night?

Once you figure out how to capture that little block of time, you can write the findings down and make 10 copies of how you will always give yourself an extra 15 minutes per day. You can be persistent in finding those extra 15 minutes, so you can keep reminding yourself that these are your "new" minutes for you to accomplish something new.

The second step requires that you write down what you want to accomplish in those 15 minutes.

A good habit will take approximately 20 days to form. Your new block of time will change your life, if you accomplish something greater in those 15 minutes!

If a man does not keep pace with his companions, perhaps it is because he hears a different drummer.
Let him step to the music which he hears, however measured or far away.

--Henry David Thoreau
Author/Naturalist
(1817-1862)

Be Different

Be unique. Be different. Stop following the crowd. Listen for the sound of that distant drum. The successful person and the average person approach life differently. The average person, it seems to me, likes to take the easy way out. It's almost as if the average person wants to get through work just to rush home to do very little, or nothing at all.

Television is often a thief of your time and can easily be the source of your losing 15 minutes a day that could be used to accomplish more worthwhile goals. Perhaps watching one less television show will create better opportunities for yourself. Why watch other people become successful when you can apply yourself to those extra 15 minutes every day?

People can too often fail because they do not "stay focused." Remember that staying focused on the small goals is the way you accomplish the final goal. Think for a moment about a movie camera. Until the lens focuses on a particular object, everything is blurry. Although you may want to accomplish many different things in unrelated fields, you may be dabbling in many fields at the same time and not putting enough energy into one goal.

Instead, remain focused, as if you are trying to line up a photo of a rose, capturing it in sharp detail. The camera lens has to stay focused or everything becomes blurry.

You must stay focused and not try to do everything at once. To hit a home run in baseball, you must have the bat make contact with the baseball at precisely the right part of the bat, hitting the right part of the ball exactly with the right force of the swing. Any deviation from these elements can result in a complete miss or a pop-up. It takes minute differences to hit the ball just right for a home run.

Focus. You may find it hard to stay focused at first. Remember this rule: a new habit takes about three weeks to form.

In a 1985 monthly publication of <u>Insight</u>, there is an article about Andrew Carnegie, the great steel maker, who was asked by a reporter, "How is it possible to have 43 millionaires working for you at the same time?"

Mr. Carnegie answered, "They weren't millionaires when they started working for me." The reporter asked, "Well, what happened?" Mr. Carnegie replied, "We believe in rewarding excellence in performance, and these men have developed themselves to the degree that they have become millionaires."

The reporter asked, "How do you develop so many people?"

Andrew Carnegie replied this way: "I develop men exactly the same way you mine gold. In order to get an ounce of gold, you move tons and tons of dirt. But you don't go looking for the dirt; you go looking for the gold."

When interviewed by <u>Success Magazine</u> in 1898 Thomas Edison was asked, "What's the first requisite for success?" And Edison answered this way: "The ability to apply your physical and mental energies to one problem incessantly without growing weary. You do something all day long, don't you? Everyone does. If you get up at 7 A.M. and go to bed at 11 P.M., you have put in 16 good hours, and it is certain with most men that they have been doing something all the time. The only trouble is that they do it about a great many things and I do it about one. If they took the time in question and applied it in one direction, to one object they would succeed."

Leadership

Why are very few people leaders? Many people are followers in general and in most all aspects of life. Many seem to follow others, much like all the mice that fall in line to follow behind the Pied Piper.

I believe many people are too shy to lead, in whatever situation they are in. The average person, when entering a department store, will follow the person who previously entered the store. People will follow other people through the same exact door, no matter that other doors are more accessible. People tend to follow the path of a predecessor. People do the same thing because it's easier that way. It takes more commitment, work, and determination to find and to independently accomplish something new and better.

In a casino, if there is an empty roulette or blackjack table, people will usually walk right by it. But as soon as one person sits down at the table, it's amazing how the table fills up with new people following the lead of the person who first sat down. Why? Maybe people think that they would miss out on something good, so they join the lone player.

It has been known that in the former Soviet Union, people were so used to standing on line that, once a line formed, other people automatically joined on the long line. They didn't want to miss out on whatever was for sale.

Who can be the leader of the pack? Anyone. With just a little imagination and determination, anyone can come up with new ideas to lead the way.

Remember, many people we know will be the followers, and will expect us to follow the followers also. I'm in no way saying this to degrade or make fun of people, but merely to bring out a point of truth. The average person is often not aware of the strong urge to "follow the crowd."

Being Different In Order To Accomplish Greater Goals

Being different means standing up, standing out, and leading. Too many people are content to be followers. Do you dare to be different?

One must plan to be different. You can start to love being different so that "being different" will become a good habit. You can make a plan and practice being different.

You do not have to be like everyone else. You can mentally note each and every time that you are different. You can go out of your way to do something that makes you stand out from the crowd.

Be different – be better! You can't miss with that attitude. With a new modified success attitude, you will become successful.

John Quincy Adams said, "If your actions inspire others to dream more, learn more, do more and become more, you are a leader."

The inventor of the disposable Gillette razor blade, King Camp Gillette, was a traveling salesman who sold bottle stoppers. He got the razor idea one morning in 1895 while shaving with a dull razor. It took 8 years of pure struggle and frustration to market the first double edge disposable shaving blade to the public. He had to find the right combination of metal alloy and tempering.

He also had to find the financial backing needed. In the process, he experienced tremendous ridicule and failure. It was almost too much to bear.

In 1903 the first Gillette blade and razor were sold to the public, and since then more than 100 billion Gillette blades have been sold.

"I didn't know enough to quit," the inventor once said. "I was a dreamer who believed in the gold at the foot of the rainbow. I dared to go where wise ones feared to tread."

Gillette had absolutely no experience in inventing, in engineering, or in working different forms of metals and alloys.

He had not the slightest idea of what he would encounter. But he had an idea, a dream, an inspiration and a belief that it could be done and, despite all the obstacles, he achieved his goal.

Don't you think there were more experienced and knowledgeable experts, engineers, and inventors than Mr. Gillette who could have invented this fantastic razor? No doubt there were thousands of people who had the potential to invent a new and better razor. What held them back? Apparently no one else had the foresight, imagination, or the burning desire to replace the antiquated shaving instrument that everyone accepted as sufficient. Others couldn't visualize a piece of metal as thin as paper, yet strong enough to slice through tough whiskers.

At times, your common sense will interfere with your creative imagination. Your common sense will tell you all the reasons you cannot do something and all those reasons are likely true. But then you have to stop to realize your brain has something greater than common sense.

We are each born with creative imagination. Successful people are the ones who have learned how to apply their creative imagination in order to achieve greater goals. Being successful can mean being more imaginative, not necessarily being smarter than someone else.

If your common sense says no, that's the time to test your options. It's your creative imagination that has the ability to overcome every it-can't-be-done attitude and common sense worry.

Consider how much any inventor has had to endure ridicule during the development stage of the invention. The criticism and the negativity from others could easily have defeated all the major inventors. Imagine the world without all the major inventions if the inventors had given up. Too many people give up on their ideas, telling themselves, "I can't do it." That amounts to accepting defeat before they have even tried.

Thomas Edison was laughed at when he tried to sell the idea of the light bulb. People did not understand the concept; they were happy using their gaslights. His skeptics kept asking, "How does Edison expect to light anything without using a flame or a fire of some kind?"

Skeptics have a difficult time in accepting change.

Thomas Edison is a great example of someone who did not give up. From his creative imagination and hard work, we have his legacy of the electric light bulb, motion pictures, the telephone transmitter, the stock ticker, the phonograph and the electric pen for the mimeograph.

Thank God, Thomas Alva Edison did not let his skeptics, his common sense, and all his failed experiments defeat him. I wonder how many times his common sense started telling him, "It can't be done." Success means you have to be willing to risk not listening to your common sense.

Alexander Graham Bell, the inventor of the telephone, had a difficult time convincing others the telephone invention would work. People accepted the telegraph as the means of communication because that already worked and people follow what works. Bell used his creative imagination to go to the next step: imagining that people could speak into a piece of metal and their voices would travel across the country over a wire in a split second.

To use your creative imagination will require research and hard work.

You can succeed in your ultimate goal if you have the conviction to persevere through all the negative attitudes and through your failed attempts.

Your goal may not come easily, but success usually comes to those who persist, those who choose to be different.

The spirit, the will to win,
and the will to excel are the
things that endure. These qualities
are so much more important than
the events that occur.

--Vince Lombardi
Football Coach
(1913-1970)

2
Time Is A Precious Gift

When it's all over, all said and done, What impact will your life have had on the world?

--John Paul Carinci

Insurance Executive

The Question of a Lifetime

Your life is such a great asset. As you grow, you learn to protect your life, to take care of your health, and to nurture your mind. But, do you really put the right effort in making the most of this gift called life? You don't have to discover a new invention or be the president of the country, but you do have the responsibility to ask yourself, Do you consciously try to make the world better?

How have you made it a better place in which to live? In what ways have you had positive, lasting effects on others? What special innovation will you be remembered for? Will people think of you as a doer, a visionary, a leader who accomplished something better? Or, will people remember you for having wasted your abilities?

These are tough questions. Most people may not want to think about these questions. The average person tends to ask, "How can I get as much as possible for me?" and seldom asks, "How can I give to the world?"

Be honest with yourself. Are you content with what you've done thus far? Have you done enough for others? What will you ultimately be remembered for? If you truly would like to change your future, you can. You simply have to be willing to modify the way you think.

17

My premise is this: You have the capacity to do great things by the use of your creative imagination.

The secret to change is, first, to tell yourself that you want to change. Tell yourself every day you want to improve something in your life. Work on small goals that lead to your greater goals.

Those who have benefited from attending Alcoholics Anonymous have had to start with an admission: "I have a problem." The admission of a problem creates the mental attitude that brings about a new result.

The first step in bringing about positive change is to admit that you want to change. Be specific about what you want to change. Will power is a tremendous tool. Once a person becomes determined to do something, and blocks out all external negative thoughts, that person usually succeeds in his or her desired goal.

The more you tell yourself that you want to improve, the more your subconscious will begin thinking of ways to achieve that goal. You can train your mind to think positively.

Your Mortality

Most of us come to admit that life is short. Once you reach the age of forty the fact that life is short sticks in your mind.You can use your own mortality as a way of staying focused.

The awareness of your mortality can even motivate you to quicken your pace of accomplishments.

You have 24 hours in every day, 168 hours in a week, and about 16 waking hours every day. That's 112 waking hours every week.

If you are a 40-year-old man with a normal life expectancy, you have approximately 16,425 more days to live, assuming you live to age 85. Women live three years longer on average. If you decided to find 20 minutes a day over a five-year period, you would accumulate about 609 hours of "extra time" to do what you wanted. Those 609 hours could change your life.

If I were to invest my 609 hours into learning to paint, don't you think after 609 hours I would be pretty knowledgeable about painting? Imagine what new things you could accomplish if you improved your life twenty minutes at a time every day.

Leo Tolstoy, the famous Russian writer, said, "Everyone thinks of changing the world, but no one thinks of changing himself."

In the entertainment field, an actor with as few as five years acting experience can become a director because of what he has learned about directing on-the-job.

In <u>Working Smarter</u>, a cassette program by Michael LeBoeuf, Ph.D., published by Nightingale Conant Corp., the following story appeared: "Charles Schwab, when he was President of Bethlehem Steel many years ago, called in Ivy Lee, a consultant, and said to him, 'Show me a way to get more things done with my time, and I'll pay you any fee within reason.' Lee replied, 'Fine. I'll give you something in 20 minutes that will step up your output at least 50%.'

With that, Lee handed Schwab a blank piece of paper and said, 'Write down the six most important things you have to do tomorrow and number them in order of importance. Now put this piece of paper in your pocket. First thing tomorrow morning look at item one and start working on it until you finish it; then do item two, and so on; do this until quitting time and don't be concerned if you've only finished one or two. You'll be working on the most important ones anyway. If you can't finish them all by this method, you couldn't have done it by any other method either, and without some system you'd probably not even have decided which was the most important.'

Then Lee said, 'Try this system every working day. After you've convinced yourself of the value of this system, have your men try it. Try it as long as you wish, then send me a check for what you think it's worth.'

Several weeks later Schwab sent Lee a check for $25,000, with a note, proclaiming the advice, 'the most profitable he'd ever followed.' The concept helped Charles Schwab earn 100 million dollars and turned Bethlehem Steel into the biggest independent steel producer in the world."

Charles Schwab thought enough of this idea to pay $25,000 for it, but only after he and his workers used it and proved it worthwhile.

Since early on in my career, I have used a similar "To Do List." I've found that the list helps me accomplish more and accomplish it faster. The to-do list keeps me focused and I avoid wasting time on the less important things.

I've presented you with a system worth $25,000, a gift for organizing your time. Try this system for four weeks. Then, look back and see how much you have accomplished. How much would you pay for such a system? I've found the system worth thousands of dollars to me over my twenty-plus years in sales.

> *Anyone who stops learning is old*
> *whether at twenty or eighty. Anyone*
> *who keeps learning stays young. The*
> *greatest thing in life is to keep your*
> *mind young.*
>
> *--Henry Ford*
> *Inventor/Automobile Manufacturer*
> *(1863-1947)*

One Sunday morning I felt shocked to see in the local newspaper an obituary of a 24-year-old man who had died in an automobile accident. He was to be married in less than a month to my cousin's daughter. I felt shock, sadness, and utter desperation in searching for a reason why we had lost the young man in a freak, arbitrary accident. I thought of my cousin's daughter, who had celebrated her wedding shower a few weeks earlier and had received beautiful gifts.

I wondered about this young man's sudden death and it finally sank in: there are no tomorrows guaranteed to any of us.

You know what you expect and what you want to happen tomorrow, but you don't know what other events will change your life, change your future, or whether you will even be alive.

Today is the only day to live, to dream, and to act.

The present time is all you have as your "guaranteed time." You need to say to yourself, "I cannot allow my dreams and goals to lie dormant inside me. From this day forward, I will write down all the things I want to accomplish. I must plan and set into motion the actions that will accomplish my great goals."

Writing Leads to Accomplishing Your Goals

Begin by writing down what you specifically want to accomplish.

No matter how complicated a project, desire, or want, write it down. Although you may be writing a rough draft, you will have begun to formulate your end goal. The act of writing your goals places the desire to accomplish this goal into your subconscious mind.

Step one: write out what you want in life. You can organize your ideas as short-term goals and long-term goals. This may be the first time you seriously set down goals. If you have already done this exercise at one point in your life, do it again. It may have been a long time since you last did this and you need to focus on your new goals.

The writing helps you to identify goals and, in turn, your creative imagination will be stimulated to find new ways to accomplish these goals.

Writing your goals is a necessary step to accomplishing them.

God gave every single human being
a certain amount of talent, and unless
you utilize that talent to the utmost
of your ability 24 hours of every day
your life, you deceive your God, your
family, and above all yourself. This is
what life is all about, this is my religion.

> *--George Allen*
> *Football Coach*
> *(1918-1990)*

3
The Little That Make All The Difference

Do your work - not just your work and
no more, but a little more for the
lavishing's sake; that little more
which is worth all the rest. And if
you suffer, as you must, do your work.
Put your heart into it, and the sky
will clear. Then out of your very doubt
and suffering will be born the supreme
joy of life.

--Dean Briggs
Spiritual Writer

No More Just An Average Person

If you look at the average worker, you will see that too many people do only what is expected of them and no more. How many people do you know who are enthusiastic about their work? Do most of the people you know only dream about getting off work in order to be free to have their "fun time?"

Since the average person will only do the minimum amount of work, you can distinguish yourself and achieve greater opportunities by investing your "extra effort." Your extra effort will develop new opportunities for you, provide you with financial rewards, and help you to excel. To excel in your field should be one of your goals.

Remember the old cartoon <u>Yogi</u> <u>Bear</u>? His motto was, "Smarter than the average bear." That's a good motto for all of us. Being average does not guarantee success. Being average is boring. Be different by being above average, and you will excel.

The real challenge is in being different.

Excel Beyond the Average

The annual New York City Marathon draws at least 20,000 runners. The race is a little over 26 miles long.

After running 26 miles, the first runner may be ahead of the second runner only by 30 seconds and 50 yards. Such a small window of time over 26 miles may make the difference between winning and losing the race. The first-place runner did a little bit extra that made all the difference in winning the race.

It's said that if the average baseball player were to get only one more hit out of every 10-15 times that he comes to bat, that player then would be guaranteed a spot in baseball's Hall Of Fame. In addition, that player would have earned millions of dollars extra over the average player. Average? Anyone can be average. Ted Williams, an outstanding player who qualified for baseball's Hall of Fame, showed what it meant not to be average. There may seem to be small differences in players, but the results are profound.

You can excel at anything, but you must be willing to make the tough choices, and put forth the extra effort.

I remember starting out as a young salesman for a major company when the vice president of the company came to our office for a sales meeting. After the meeting, I walked up to him and shook his hand. Before letting go of our handshake, I said, "Mr. Posa, I'm going to be one of your district managers one day. I don't know exactly when, but you are going to promote me to that position one day."

Two years later I fulfilled that prophecy I had made to him and the promise I made to myself to advance quickly in the company. At age 27, I became the company's youngest manager.

I knew I would be promoted in the company because I was totally consumed by the desire to be a district manager. Every day I thought about it. I pictured myself as the manager of the agency and acted as if I'd already had the position. I knew in my heart I would be promoted; I just didn't know when.

When you have a burning desire to accomplish something, nothing can stop you. You accept the hardships and disappointments. You separate yourself from the average workers by your consuming desire to reach your goal.

Small Efforts Can Pay Off In Big Ways

Assuming you get eight hours of sleep, imagine if you could get by with 7 1/2 hours of sleep from age 35. Over a lifetime you would end up with an extra 7,720 hours of waking time. Can you imagine how much more you could achieve in your lifetime with all that time?

A little extra effort can result in greater rewards.

You may have to start by sleeping five minutes less every day, until you are comfortable with that goal. After that goal is achieved, you can get up another five minutes earlier. Gradually, you will be giving yourself anywhere from ten minutes to thirty minutes of "extra time" that will help you reach a greater goal.

If you heat water to 211 degrees Fahrenheit, you simply have hot water. By heating the water to 212 degrees Fahrenheit, you have boiling water. That one degree makes the difference that can move locomotives, and steamships, while also even melting certain compounds.

Are you operating at the 211 degree level? Are you willing to give that extra one-degree effort? With just a little bit extra effort and creative imagination, you could improve yourself and the world around you.

Horse races, sometimes, are won "by a nose." In a photo finish, that may mean that the first place horse was a hundredth or one-thousandth of a second faster than another horse.

Roger Maris, a former New York Yankees ballplayer and a member of the Baseball Hall of Fame, became famous when he broke Babe Ruth's home run record. In 1961, Maris hit 61 home runs, breaking Ruth's home run record of 60 home runs held since 1927.

In 1982, Rickey Henderson guaranteed himself a spot in Baseball's Hall of Fame by setting a new record for stolen bases. He stole 130 bases in one season, breaking Lou Brock's old record of 118, set in 1974.

Since the first Olympic games many centuries ago in Athens, Greece, records have been shattered and new ones made. The brain often wills the body to accomplish the record-breaking feat.

The Mental Attitude To Doing More

Sports records have been broken by those willing to make the extra effort.

In <u>Success</u> <u>Through</u> <u>A</u> <u>Positive</u> <u>Mental</u> <u>Attitude,</u> a self-help book by Napoleon Hill and W. Clement Stone, a story about Roger Bannister appeared: "In 1954 Roger Bannister set a new world record by running the one-mile race in less than 4 minutes. It had never been done in the history of track and field competition. How did he do it when no one else in history could do it? Here's how: his trainer Dr. Cureton came up with a training plan of action: 'Number one, Train the whole body. Number two, push yourself to the limit of endurance, extending the limit with each workout.' Dr.

Cureton said, 'The art of record-breaking is the ability to take more out of yourself than you've got.'

"Roger Bannister trained in the following manner: Since the quarter of the mile can be run faster per quarter than the full mile, he trained so that each quarter of the mile was a race in itself, and if he ran them at quarter mile paces, he could put four of them together and run the mile faster than he normally could.

"Bannister would run all out a quarter of a mile at a time to the point of collapse, and each time he would push the point of collapse a little further along the way. Well, on May 6, 1954 Roger Bannister ran the mile in 3 minutes 59.6 seconds, the fastest time in the world."

After Bannister broke the four-minute mile, many other runners started breaking the four-minute mile barrier. They had learned that they had to develop the power of positive thinking in order to produce greater results. Once they learned to set their minds to accomplish a new goal, more and more runners began learning that their minds could be used to help them break the old records.

Your mind is capable of many more things. All you have to do is break through your own mental limitations.

It was William James who said, "The first and most important factor at the beginning of any project is belief."

The Power Deep Inside

I believe your subconscious mind stores information you can use to be successful. Use that information by following Dr. Cureton's advice and take yourself "to the limit of endurance." With a little bit of extra time and effort invested in yourself, you will surprise yourself at what you will achieve.

Did you ever notice in sports, such as baseball, the American pastime, that many times, if a team scores two quick runs on another team, the opposing team coincidentally catches up by scoring back those two runs themselves? In basketball, one team will seem to score 10 points quickly. Amazingly, the other team rebounds with a surge of 8-10 points quickly.Have you seen in hockey where both teams will go scoreless most of the game? When one team scores, the opposing team will rebound with a goal to tie the score. Why is this so common?

Your subconscious mind is a great powerhouse to help you do whatever you have to do. The subconscious mind is constantly sending thoughts to your conscious mind. I believe your subconscious mind can force you to accomplish greater results.

I am convinced that if we were to take a baseball team into a room midway through a game, even if that team was winning the game, we could convince them through hypnosis that they were losing by 5 runs. At that point, the subconscious mind of each player would start sending signals to his conscious mind that he had to play harder in order to win the game. There is an amazing power going on in the subconscious that can force the conscious mind and eventually the body to perform either aggressively or lackadaisically.

Since you know this power exists, be very careful what you feed your mind. I believe that your subconscious mind is like a sponge, absorbing information, only to reappear later as positive or negative impulses.

Don't let your subconscious draw in negative thoughts. Someone once said, "We are what we think about."

What are you feeding your mind lately? Remember the computer user's phrase, "Garbage in, garbage out" can hold true for your mind. The better phrase to live by every day is "Positive in, positive outcome."

Never forget: A successful person never lives a nonchalant life!

Do more than exist, live.

Do more than touch, feel.

Do more than look, observe.

Do more than read, absorb.

Do more than hear, listen.

Do more than think, ponder.

Do more than talk, say something.

--John H. Rhoades

Poet/Philosopher

4
A Positive Attitude

*Nothing can stop the man with the right
mental attitude from achieving his goal;
nothing on earth can help the man with
the wrong mental attitude.*

> *--Thomas Jefferson*
> *3rd United States President*
> *(1743-1826)*

The Creative Fire In You

Don't let anyone stomp on your dreams, kill your inspirations, or put out your fire of aggressive creativity with gratuitous negativity.

Inspiration is the creative fire of phenomenal ideas.

Thankfully, the great inventors through the ages were not quitters. They did not let negative public opinion sway them from accomplishing their endeavors.

You are capable of great ideas. What is your great idea? Could one of your ideas become a useful invention? Could one of your ideas be turned into a great book? Could one of your ideas help save the lives of millions of people? You have such great potential. Just dream it, be consumed by it, and it will be yours.

You may have decided you would rather forget your idea than subject yourself to others laughing at you and embarrassing you. Ridicule from others is not easy to accept and something you don't want to hear. You become scared about your ideas when others tell you "you're wasting your time."

Do you remember the Dick Tracy detective comics in the newspapers years ago? Remember how Dick Tracy would talk into his wristwatch telephone? It sounded crazy then, but the idea became a reality once an inventor developed the microchips needed for such a telephone. To the average person, the idea seemed too big and too difficult to comprehend. How could a big telephone be reduced to the size of a wristwatch? For the person who uses his creative imagination, the questions became, 'How can I miniaturize the telephone circuitry and make it work?' and 'How can I make the telephone work over the airwaves without a connecting wire?'

"Dream it; believe in it; be consumed with it; and it will come to fruition."

Thanks to a lot of inventions in technology and satellite communications by many people and companies, you can now talk to people around the world from a small portable phone just like Dick Tracy.

Conceive, Believe, and Achieve

Notice how the airplane looks like a bird. Man observed, conceived, believed, and then achieved flying according to the same principles by which birds fly.

The first television set came out in the 1940's. If I told people in 1940 that I was going to invent a one-inch by one-inch color television, they would have laughed behind my back by calling me the biggest fool on earth. That miniature color television set now exists. And not only that, you can now have your color video telephone to go along with your miniature color television.

I've become aware how miniaturized everything has become. Our western culture has become a culture of miniaturized, technological devices. Inventors, scientists, and researchers have used their creative imagination to find ways to put volumes of books on a CD, to scan billions of bits of information in less than a second, and to incorporate whole libraries of books into small memory boards. Researchers, applying their creative imagination, are trying to develop future computers that use atoms for storing information, not just chips. These new inventions will lead to further miniaturizing computers, cameras, telephones, and all kinds of electronic and communication products.

You can certainly see that technology keeps changing and improving. If you don't start working on your creative ideas now, someone else may have the persistence to accomplish what you wanted to accomplish.

Thank God there are individuals who have the vision, determination, and drive to forge ahead through failure after failure. You may only have the mental picture of a given idea or invention, but that mental picture can be enough to keep you working on your idea. Thousands of new inventions are being patented every day. When will people see the completion of your idea?

Imagine somewhere that there should be a monument to lost ideas. It's not a junk heap. It's the should-have-been heap. It's a pile of the best ideas that were never tried or fulfilled. It's the unfulfilled patents or never-written books or never-created ideas because somebody was afraid to try or somebody ridiculed the idea to death. Is that where you want your ideas to end up?

Look at Henry Ford, who in his early years began working on inventing a gas-driven engine. Ford had a study done by a leading college to see if the gas engine could be invented. After extensive study, the college's technical department determined that the idea could not be done. A piston could not be made to move by gasoline-ignited power.

Henry Ford still believed he could build such an engine. He purchased his own parts and with help from his wife, he got the first makeshift piston powered by droplets of gasoline ignited by a spark. The rest is history. The horses and the steam engines of the day were gradually replaced with the internal combustion engine in the early 1900s. Henry Ford then developed the first successful automobile assembly line, building cars faster than anyone had imagined. A man with vision, determination, and fortitude, Henry Ford proved himself a true visionary who would not let his ideas be extinguished by the negativity and ridicule of others.

Steps To Securing Your Vision

First, don't stop yourself from dreaming; dreaming is the starting point.

Second, don't let others stifle your creative imagination. Your ideas are greatest when you feel free to use your imagination.

Third, don't let your problems stop you. It's been said that going to sleep with a problem can be a good thing. During your sleep, your brain can quietly think about the problem. You can actually wake up with a new solution to your problem. Allow your subconscious mind to work on the problem.

Your mind is a tremendous tool when given the opportunity to prove itself.

Researchers believe people use only about 5% of the brain's capacity. That leaves 95% room for your creative imagination. You can use that extra part of your brain to keep telling yourself, "I'm going to do it! I'm going to do it!

I'm going to be successful!" Let yourself be different and *think*! Use your brain and *think*! There is so much more you can be doing with your brain capacity than you imagined!

Wilber and Orville Wright first flew a heavier-than-air machine in 1903. But they were successful only after repeated failures. The average person around them dismissed the idea that any human could fly. Once the Wright brothers proved flight in machines to be possible, the world quickly picked up the pace and improved the design. Today, we've gone from flying a few feet off the ground to flying into space.

It amazes me how it takes a major breakthrough before all the rest of the people in the world believe what is possible.

It's always easier to say, with the average person, that something is impossible than to use your creative imagination, work hard, and let your subconscious bring about a breakthrough, a new invention, or to turn a new idea into reality.

What the mind of man can conceive
and believe it can achieve, through
a positive mental Attitude.

> *--Napoleon Hill*
> *Motivational Author*
> *(1883-1970)*

There are some race horses who can not run a good race because they're distracted by the commotion at the starting gate. The trainers usually try to fix the problem by putting blinders on a horse's eyes to block out the distractions and keep the horse focused directly in front. The blinders in some horses can make a difference between winning and losing a race.

All of us occasionally need to put on mental blinders to block out too much negativity and skepticism. You don't need bad comments, bad thoughts, and people emphasizing your failures at a time when you are very close to succeeding.

You have to keep focused, stay positive, and eliminate dwelling on any comments from others that are not helping you to find solutions you need to succeed.

Anyone criticizing you should also try to help you find success. The last thing you need is to have one or more people telling you what a failure you are. You can always find someone who will want to kill your idea, inspiration, perseverance, and drive. Remember, success is not easy to achieve. It's a long road that many refuse to walk.

As for the negative people around you, you will have to work around them or avoid them. You don't want their negativity to register inside and overpower your subconscious.

I believe most of the great inventors and achievers have had to use mental blinders and have had to get past a lot of negative comments. Just as a bodybuilder works hard to build up his or her muscles, so too, you have to build up your mind to learn to sidestep all the negative influences and stay focused on your goal of success.

Remember:

1- Determine clearly what it is you want to accomplish.

2- Write it down in detail.

3- Write down why you wish to accomplish this goal.

4- Write down how long it will take to accomplish the goal. Write down exactly the time needed and how you will invest yourself daily and weekly to reach your goal.

5- Write out a complete statement to the effect that under no circumstances will you allow anyone to alter your attitude toward the accomplishment of the desired goal.

Success seems to be connected with action. Successful people keep moving. They make mistakes, but they don't quit.

--Conrad Hilton
Hotel Owner
(1887-1979)

I read an inspirational story that I will never forgot. It came from the aforementioned <u>Success</u> <u>Through</u> <u>A</u> <u>Positive</u> <u>Mental</u> <u>Attitude</u> by Napoleon Hill and W. Clement Stone. They told a story about a farmer named Milo C. Jones, who for most of his life had owned a small farm in Wisconsin. He had been barely able to provide enough for his family and himself year after year, never making a great living.

One year Jones was struck down with paralysis that left him bedridden and incapacitated. Though paralyzed, he had a very sharp mind. He believed in being responsible and strengthened his determination not to quit or give up on life. Jones knew he had to do something to help his family. He called his family together around his bed for a meeting at which time he told them his new plan of action.

"I am no longer able to work with my hands, so I have decided to work with my mind. Everyone of you can, if you will, take the place of my hands, feet, and physical body. Let's plant every tillable acre of our farm in corn. Then let's raise pigs and feed them the corn. Let's slaughter the pigs while they are young and tender and convert them into sausages. Then we can package and sell the sausages under our own brand name. We'll sell them in retail stores around the country. They'll sell like hot cakes," Jones told his family enthusiastically.

This was the founding idea that began Jones' Little Pig Sausages. The family members followed the plan and the sausages sold in stores and the business thrived. That was in 1889 and the recipe is still used today.

Milo C. Jones could have given up on life very easily and nobody would have blamed him because of his disability. But Jones was a man who did not want to lie in bed doing nothing. He took what he had left, his mind, and used it to the very best of his ability. He used his creative imagination. I'm convinced that his mind actually got sharper after he became paralyzed.

A blind person learns to hear differently than a person who has the ability to see. People have learned to work through their physical limitations without being defeated by the limitations. We may call it *compensating* for the limitation, but it's more than plain compensation. There's a new way of thinking. The limitation forces some people to think differently in spite of the limitation.

All of us have limitations of some type – physical or financial. Your goal is to achieve your dreams in spite of your limitations. Limitations are no longer limitations; they are no longer an excuse for failure. Limitations are simply a set of problems that you have to solve in order to go forward to find success. Your creative imagination is the spark, and hard work is the piston driving you forward. You can achieve your goals in spite of your problems.

Imagine what you could do if you went from using the five percent of your brain to using ten percent of your brain. Every percentage point that you increase in using your brain could yield incredible results in your life.

It's our attitude at the beginning of a difficult task, that will more than anything else determine it's outcome.

-- William James
Psychologist
(1842-1910)

5
The Miracle of Life

*Thank God every morning when you get up
that you have something to do which must
be done, whether you like it or not, being
forced to work, and forced to do your best,
will breed in you a hundred virtues which
the idle never know.*

> *--Charles Kingsley*
> *Author/Clergy*
> *(1819-1875)*

Your Uniqueness Creates Your Success

As you get older, you most likely learn to appreciate life more - the miracle of life, the latent powers within the mind, and the meaning of your own distinctive personality.

While sitting in the car waiting for my wife, I noticed a flying insect on the window next to me. It appeared to be no bigger than the eye of a large sewing needle. I watched it walk slowly up the window. As I studied it, I thought, All the different varieties of life on this planet are amazing.

I noticed this miniscule insect had half of its body covered by wings. I was always intrigued how insects and birds could fly and defy gravity. This insect had lightweight wings, which were strong enough to carry the insect away quickly.

I had an epiphany about the miracle of life. Although this insect was not the smallest form of life on earth, I had been mesmerized thinking about this creature with its own heart, brain, nervous system, lungs, stomach, arteries, and, oh yes, six legs. That insect impressed me.

I've read that the human body has approximately 70,000 miles of blood vessels. When the heart beats, it circulates the blood through the entire system of vessels once every minute. Another amazing fact is that the human brain weighs only about three pounds, yet it holds an estimated eighty trillion electrical cells.

Each One Of Us Represents A Miracle

Consider how unique each one of us is. Even identical twins have some differences between them. If you don't have an identical twin, it can be said that there is no one else exactly like you. Unlike computers, which may be identical computing systems, you interpret the world through your brain and that brain develops its own personality, the mechanism that helps you understand and react to the world around you.

To become who you are, it took one of about 5 million microscopic sperm cells to reach the egg. Your personality, everything about you, and your potential were carried in that one sperm.

Millions of other sperm cells died searching for the egg, while one sperm cell combined with the egg that gave you life, resulting in your extraordinary uniqueness.

You are a miracle. In fact, childbirth is a miracle because we all had to survive about nine months in the womb in order to be strong enough to be born into the world. The chances of you being born were one in 5 million, based on the estimated number of sperm. Don't ever feel sorry for yourself if you haven't yet won the lottery; you've already won the lottery by being born!

Using All Your Talents to the Fullest

Dennis Waitley wrote the following story in <u>Insight</u>: "The Scriptures tell of a story of a master of a wealthy estate who gave some of his fortune to three of his servants. To the first servant he gave five talents; to the second, three talents; to the third servant he gave one talent. A talent in those days was a measure of money. He told the three servants to 'cherish and utilize to the fullest what had been given.' And after one year he would check with them to see what they had done.

"The first servant invested his money in different businesses. The second servant bought materials and made things to sell. The third servant took his talent and hid it and saved it. After one year the master saw that the first servant, through his investing, had now 25 talents. The second servant had built his up to 15 talents, which made the master happy. So he asked the third servant what had become of his one talent. The servant exclaimed, 'I was afraid to misuse the talent, so I carefully hid it. Here it is!

I am now giving it back to you in the same condition as when you gave it to me!' The master was very mad. 'Thou wicked and slothful servant. How dare you not use the gift that I gave you?'"

Here is an encouraging estimate: people in America can often live to be 85 or 90. Today's newborn will have the benefits of medical science that will enable them to live to be 100 to 110.

We are very fortunate today to be able to live long, healthy, and productive lives. Our forbearers often died from fever, pneumonia, and even childbirth, which killed many women and children. Imagine living centuries ago when a good life meant living only into your thirties. Imagine ending your opportunities by age thirty.

The person who is 70 today is often healthier than a person 60 years old who lived in the 16th and 17th centuries. Today, it's not unheard of for a 75-year-old to run New York City's 26-mile marathon and to finish. Though you always have dangers around you that can cut your life short, the statistics are in your favor to live a healthy and active life into old age.

Can you appreciate the fact that you will probably have more time on this great earth than your ancestors? Or do you waste and undervalue your life? Do you wish for more free time? Most of us do, but what would you do in your free time to find greater success?

While growing up, I can remember my father working three jobs to support our family. I don't remember him ever relaxing or hanging around the house. He worked hard. I learned of his hard work when I used to go with him after school to clean oil burners. Believe me, he earned every cent he was paid.

In many ways, most of us have it so much better than our parents, grandparents, and ancestors. Life is considered more comfortable. In some instances, people have more free time and all of us have more options as to what we may want to do in our free time. How will you choose to use this extra time you have?

I saw something on television that really shocked me. It is good to be shocked occasionally to prevent us from taking life for granted. A reality check.

On this particular show, I saw a story about a thirty-five year old man who had been born without legs. It appeared that his torso was flat right below his waist. This birth defect, which would be devastating to anyone, did not stop him from living a normal life. I watched as he walked on the palms of his hands. He walked on his hands right to the edge of a pool, flipped himself in, and started swimming with his arms.

While swimming, he appeared as a normal person with legs. Then he reached up, pulled himself up and out of the pool. Using his hands, he walked right over to a chaise lounge at poolside and pulled himself onto the center of the chaise lounge. I sat transfixed, wondering what else this man could do. The program went on to show him in the kitchen, where he pulled himself onto a chair and then onto the kitchen counter in order to eat his meal.

Finally, I watched this unusual man fulfill his desire to be an automobile mechanic by actually climbing into the engine compartment to work on a car. I could not help but respect his sheer determination to live his life as any fully functioning person would.

If you apply greater determination, imagine what you could accomplish. Do you appreciate your own life? Do you appreciate what you could become with a small amount of that man's determination? Or, are you busy making too many excuses why you can't be successful? Do you realize the awesome power your mind possesses? You can become anything you dream.

Some people can only move the muscles in their face. Some of these quadriplegic individuals can only use a stick hanging out of their mouths to touch the keys of a computer, yet, some of these people have written articles and books. They communicate with loved ones through the computer, if they cannot speak. They have shown the rest of us what can be accomplished, as long as their minds can still function. These paralyzed people always inspire and motivate me. Knowing what they're accomplishing helps me to stop making excuses and to start working harder on my goals.

As Ben Franklin said, "Don't put off till tomorrow, what can be done today."

You can do something greater, but it requires you not to wait to get started. Life is giving you a unique opportunity to do something great in this world.

Write down your thoughts. Once you have written down your thoughts, the ideas become more real. They get etched into your mind, keeping you motivated to carry out your goal.

John Paul Carinci

Well done is better than well said.

> *--Ben Franklin*
> *Statesman*
> *(1706-1790)*

6
It's A Great Day To Be Alive

The quality of a person's life is in direct proportion to their commitment to excellence regardless of their chosen field of endeavor.

--Vince Lombardi
Football Coach
(1913-1970)

You Can Make Life Positive

You can have a fantastic and successful life on earth. Avoid the negative people who complain that life is a major task to get through. We've occasionally all shared those feelings temporarily, but those negative attitudes will never help us to succeed. Remember: positive attitudes into your mind will equal positive attitudes going out.

Real living means enjoying life and finding ways to make life better for others too.

Work on developing an attitude that makes you wake up happy in the mornings and get started on your program for success.

In America, we have an abundance of food, water, housing, and some of the best medical care in the world. Most all of us can find work and, if we can't, the government offers assistance to the less fortunate.

Still, life is often challenging. It may even be stressful due to our hectic schedules.

Depending on your financial situation, you can indulge in many choices: eat all day; play hooky from school; catch a plane to Paris; or even travel to Alaska to disappear from society. The point is you have any number of freedoms to do so much. You are free to quit your job today and find a new job or career. The choice is yours. Sadly, anyone is also free to develop mostly negative attitudes. Lives can be destroyed by choosing negative attitudes. As you can see, freedom means choosing between positive and negative attitudes every day.

Freedom is a blessing we all have.

In fact, why don't you take three days off from work right now? Why don't you drive in a whole new direction and see a new state and some new towns? Study the people you meet. Learn a lot of new ideas from others and from what you see and experience. Observe life in a new place. Make it a research expedition to refresh your mind and your imagination.

Look at the power you possess. You have more options to do what you want, especially living in America. It seems at times that immigrants appreciate America more than America's own citizens. Many immigrants come from countries where they had less freedom. They see America as a place where dreams come true, even if it means they have to make sacrifices in order to succeed.

In the movie, *It's A Wonderful Life*, James Stewart plays a character who seems to get a raw deal his whole life. He always comes in last and gives much more than he ever gets. One day he wants to end it all and commit suicide. He wishes he was never born. But, when he was shown what life would be like for everyone he knew if he were never born, he changes his mind. He wants to remain alive at any cost. He doesn't want to trade in his life once he realizes how many lives his life has touched, changed, and affected positively. He cannot believe how truly valuable his life has been. It's a great movie and carries a great message.

Our lives, no matter how simple, touch and enrich so many other lives. Your life is bigger than you think and your abilities to make great things happen in your life are far greater than you can ever imagine.

In his book, <u>Long Time No See</u>, Dr. No–Yong Park writes, "It is not difficult to find the way to happiness. If you want to enjoy sunshine, first suffer some rain or snow. If you want to enjoy a mild spring, first suffer a cold, bleak winter. If you want to enjoy a good vacation, study and work hard... and earn it. If you want to enjoy a hearty meal, first work hard and burn up your energy and grow hungry...."

On the subject of happiness, Dr. Park writes, "Here's a statement of what a Korean boy thought happiness meant to him. It appeared in one of Abigail Van Buren's columns. 'Happiness is no longer having to roam the streets of Seoul, begging for food, sleeping in doorways and under bridges or being cold, hungry or dirty. Happiness is having an

American believe in me enough to take me in, give me my first real meal in years, buy my first pair of socks, and leather shoes, and underwear, and give me a bed where I could sleep between sheets, let me see my first TV and give me the first security I have ever known. Happiness means being adopted and coming to the United States. Happiness is the opportunity to attend school again for the first time in three years. Happiness is becoming an American citizen and making my new parents proud of me.'"

A Positive Daily Attitude

Tomorrow, bright and early, I want you to celebrate this theme: "It's A Great Day To Be Alive." No matter your age, think about how great it is to be alive. Think about all the good things you want to do today.

There's a story about a young man who was deeply disturbed by the fact that he was not successful. He felt that his life was worthless, that he was useless and might as well give up on life now. Someone heard the man's story and it is said that he asked the man, "If your life is worthless would you sell your eyesight, while alive, for one million dollars?" Of course, the man refused and finally realized that he had so much to be thankful for, that his eyesight alone was priceless, and that many others were blind. This man realized through this scenario that he had no right feeling pity for himself, not with all he had going for him.

I was in Atlantic City a few years ago walking along the famous boardwalk, breathing in the fresh ocean air. While walking past all the stores, I came across a woman playing an electric piano.

She did it in an extraordinary way, without having arms or legs. She was lying flat on a type of hospital bed and playing the electric piano with her tongue. Her tongue of all things!

If I hadn't seen her with my own eyes, I would have thought she was playing with all ten fingers. I respected her for her accomplishments, but I felt, too, a sense of guilt for having ever felt sorry for myself.

Here was a woman with disabilities, confronting me, with all my latent abilities, and making me question when I would start applying myself better in life. As people tossed money in her bucket next to her rolling bed, I thought about how she faced life and how it was time for me to face life even better with my arms, legs, and brain intact.

I tried to picture myself in this woman's place. I don't know that if I were in her situation, I could put myself on public display and play an electric piano with my tongue.

I admired her accomplishments, dedication, and ability to play the piano quite well.

Remember the motto: "It's A Great Day To Be Alive."

If you put that theme into practice, you should celebrate life more often. Invite people over for an impromptu party. Take your wife or family out on the town. Feel good about yourself. Remember how unique you are. Out of the billions of people in the world, no one can think and feel exactly like you. You are the most important person ever born. Celebrate life by being more successful. Look for your greatness. Find and develop the unique "you" in your life every day.

It gives me great pleasure indeed to see the stubbornness of an incorrigible nonconformist warmly acclaimed.

--Albert Einstein
Physicist
(1879-1955)

The following saying from an unknown author is very appropriate: "There are two days in every week about which we should not worry - two days which should be kept free from an apprehension. One of these days is yesterday with its mistakes and cares, its aches and pains, its faults and blunders. Yesterday has passed forever beyond our control. All the money in the world cannot bring back yesterday. We cannot undo a single act we performed; we cannot erase a single word we said; yesterday is gone!

The other day we should not worry about is tomorrow with its possible adversities, its burdens, its large promise and poor performance. Tomorrow also is beyond our immediate control.

Tomorrow's sun will rise either in splendor or behind a mask of clouds, but it will rise! Until it does, we have no stake in tomorrow, for it is as yet unborn.

That leaves only one day - today.

Any man can fight the battles of just one day. It is only when you and I add the burdens of these two awful eternities-yesterday and tomorrow, that we break down! It is not the experience of today that drives men mad, it is remorse or bitterness for something which happened yesterday, and dread of what tomorrow will bring.

Let us, therefore, journey but one day at a time!"

Dr. Robert Schuller, minister, author, and lecturer on positive thinking, told a story in Insight about his father and how his father's attitudes have remained with him to this day. Schuller, born and raised on a farm in Iowa in the 1930s, lived during a very difficult time for farmers. In one year, his father would normally harvest 10 wagons of corn from their farm, but in one particularly bad year his father harvested only half a wagon. Schuller remembers his father's feelings at the time this way: "I'll never forget how, that night, seated at the dinner table, his calloused hands folded in prayer, my father looked up and thanked God. He said, 'I thank you, God, that I have lost nothing, I got a half a wagon load back. I have regained the seed I planted in the springtime.'

"His attitude of gratitude was that he had lost nothing."

In another example of his father's "Attitude of Gratitude," Schuller tells of the time a tornado hit their home without any warning, and how they all managed to escape in the family car without harm, but the tornado did destroy all nine of their buildings on the farm.

The next night at a gathering in the country church he heard his father pray: "Oh God, I thank you that not a life was lost, not a human bone was broken. We have lost nothing that cannot be recaptured, regained and replaced. And through the storm, oh God, we have kept everything that would have been irreplaceable - the lives of the children and our own faith."

His father's "Attitude of Gratitude" is what drove this man to rebuild aggressively and with a conviction, when other men might have collapsed emotionally under the circumstances. This type of upbringing stays with a person for the rest of his life.

Your convictions and outlook can shape another's personality. So be careful of how you display yourself to others. Negative attitudes can ruin someone else's life. Positive attitudes can help to promote someone into greatness. Your attitudes, one way or another, will change another person's life forever.

There is little difference in people,
but that little difference makes a big
difference. The little difference is
attitude. The big difference is whether
it is positive or negative.

> *--W. Clement Stone*
> *Motivational Author*
> *(1902-2002)*

7
The Mind Over The Body

*Self-esteem is the key to success or failure.
Self-esteem, more than any other single factor,
determines how high in life we are likely to rise,
emotionally, financially, creatively, spiritually.
So in this world, the first love affair that we
have to consummate successfully is a love affair
with ourselves.*

> *--Nathaniel Branden*
> *Psychologist, Author*

Examples of the Mind's Power

The human mind controls the body. The body will accomplish whatever the mind tells it to. The power of the mind is a mystery that still baffles the experts.

One morning I woke up approximately 30 seconds before the alarm went off at 4:30 A.M. I can remember thinking, "This is fantastic." I had a very important appointment that morning, so before going to sleep the night before I told myself, I must get up at 4:30 A.M.

What amazed me is that I woke up at precisely the right time, although I never get up at 4:30 A.M. The mind, when instructed in the proper way, can carry out many commands.

Remember when you tried to recall someone's last name or something else and you couldn't? You went on with your business and some time later that name or what you wanted to remember popped into your mind. Without realizing it, you ordered your subconscious mind to remember the name. While you were busy doing other things with your conscious mind, your subconscious mind was busy reviewing billions of bits of memory information in a very small part of your brain.

Some of the best examples of how powerful our minds are and how our minds control our body are given by Norman Cousins, at the time a professor of Medical Humanities at the School of Medicine at the University of California, Los Angeles. The following stories by Norman Cousins appeared in <u>Insight</u>.

Cousins tells of an incident that happened in Los Angeles at a football game at Monterey Park. Four or five people were reported to be ill with symptoms of food poisoning. The doctor in charge, after questioning these people, became concerned that the soft drink dispensers might be contaminated. Not wanting to spread the sickness, he had the stadium make an announcement to all the fans, informing them of the possible food poisoning and for them not to consume any more of the dispensed beverages.

"Well you can just imagine what happened. Perfectly healthy fans started to feel faint, sick, pass out to such a point that ambulances were called from five hospitals to transport hundreds of people to the emergency rooms and hundreds of others went to their own doctors.

All the supposed sick had the same symptoms of the first four, the stomach pains, nausea, dizziness. It appeared that a major bacteria was consumed by hundreds of the fans, but the moment it was confirmed that neither the soft drinks nor dispenser were contaminated everyone suddenly got better with no more symptoms."

Norman Cousins explained, "How is it possible that just words in the air could be converted into specific illness? What is it about the human mind that can process sounds into disease? If words can make us ill, is it barely possible that words can make us better?"

Cousins speaks about the brain and how it produces 34 basic chemicals which produce combinations of thousands of mixtures. With certain stimulation, it can produce actual healing of the body, while stress can produce the chemicals that harm the body.

Some researchers believe that laughter can stimulate the brain to produce the right mixture of chemicals that are very beneficial to the healing of the individual.

What about people who retire with no active lifestyles, those who seem to waste away with no challenges, no goals, and nothing to occupy their lives? Many of these individuals mysteriously become sick or senile. Could it be that they are missing the stimulation of the proper chemicals in their brains to keep them healthy? Then there are those people who are active into their eighties and nineties and whose minds are sharp.

What have you been feeding yourself lately? Many people are concerned today about the food they eat. We are told to read every label carefully to avoid taking in too much fat, cholesterol, and sodium.

It seems we are always trying to eat foods that are healthier. My question to you is: "What have you been feeding your mind lately?" Just like your body, your mind has to be fed information. Your mind reacts to what it is fed.

Feeding your mind positive, stimulating ideas creates a sharp, creative mind. Feeding your mind negative thoughts creates negative thinking.

Exercise has been proven to be essential to maintaining a healthy body, but exercise also keeps our minds alert and positive because we feel better about ourselves. Exercise also releases the chemicals and hormones, which are the ones that make us "feel good."

One of the basic exercises you can do is walk. Some experts say walking is one of the best exercises because it is not nearly as stressful on the joints as running. Walking allows you to use nearly every muscle in the body without straining your body. Walking can be slow or fast, for short distances or long and can even be done in your local mall early in the morning.

*If we want to be something special, then
we've got to do something special.*

--John Paul Carinci

To Improve Yourself

Make up your mind this moment to start changing. Remember a new habit needs 20 days of forced repetition to become permanent.

Write down in a list of what you want to do and when you want to do it. Make it the same time of the day each time you do it and post the schedule everywhere you possibly can so you'll see it no less than 10 times every day. This is how you can start a new exercise program and stick to it.

When asked, many people have a desire to change something about themselves. The changes often include wanting to be more healthy, more positive, more successful, more attractive, and the list goes on and on.

By *giving up* something, you can be better off. If you give up smoking, your lungs become more healthy. Depending on your weight, if you lose twenty pounds or more, your whole body may improve. When your body is healthier, you gain more energy and live longer. You have to be willing to give up what you are now doing that is not right in order *to gain* more success and a healthier, happier life. If you took two bricks, strapped one to each of your shoulders, and walked around with the extra weight for the entire day, you would feel like dropping dead. This is some of the extra weight many people are carrying on their bodies. Once you lose the *unnecessary* weight, you will always wonder why you carried that extra body weight for so long.

Your mind can keep you healthy or it can bring on death. After the death of a spouse, some survivors give up on life and soon pass away themselves. They may have died prematurely out of sadness, loneliness, or simply giving up on life.

Doctors claim that people who think they're sick are very difficult to deal with. Some people have convinced themselves that they have some illness to the point that they mimic the symptoms associated with that illness.

Earl Nightingale, the well-known lecturer and researcher, said, "The only thing unique about the human being is our mind; all other things can be found in a donkey or another animal." How true! He also said something very profound: "Most people tiptoe through life to get safely to death."

The Brain's Amazing Powers

The mind is a wonderful, amazing, complicated organ and the one thing you never want to lose. If you cannot think clearly or if your mind cannot understand the world around you, your senses and your limbs lose their meaning.

Because of sickness, accidents, or the misuse of drugs and chemicals, some people have lost the partial use of their brains. It is a terrible thing to lose a fully functioning brain, which gives you your mobility, communication skills, analytical abilities, and personality.

There's a popular saying, "Use it or lose it." That saying holds true for the brain. I know of one man who is living this advice. He is well over ninety and still practices law. His son, an attorney, is in his seventies and practices law with his father.

We've all felt sick from time to time and we've all consulted a doctor. Many people feel sick with symptoms such as chest pain, back pain, and general fatigue. But after the doctor gives them a checkup, various tests, and listens to their heart, the symptoms that prompted the visit miraculously disappear. All of a sudden they feel great. They suddenly have a new-found energy and everything is all right. Their disposition and attitude improve dramatically. Why? What makes such a dramatic change take place? What creates such a total turn around from worry to happiness?

It is known that the brain can release a proper mix of chemicals to cure viruses and even cancer. If you were to cut yourself, the brain will release a mix of chemicals that begin the healing process.

The brain has its own abilities to run on autopilot, to keep you alive, if you are unconscious or in a coma. Unbelievably, if your body were completely submerged in cold water, the brain knows to slow down your heart rate to almost nothing. This is why some drowning victims, submerged for 20 minutes or longer, have been brought back to life. The brain has an amazing power to operate on its own.

When threatened or scared, the body receives a shot of adrenaline released by the brain for instant alertness, energy, and power not normally available. We've all heard stories of people who were able to lift cars, pianos, or other heavy objects off of accident victims because the brain released large amounts of adrenaline into the body to meet the emergency situation.

I believe the mind also has the power to make us sick. The mind can ultimately shut down the body. We have all heard stories of how a person seems to die because that person lost the desire to live. Our mind, if it believes something to be true, will do all it can to bring about the expected results, no matter how difficult the task.

Here's an example of how the brain can influence the body: there are prescriptions available for the purpose of making hair grow for people with thinning or bald heads. One of these drugs, a topical solution, had to be applied to the affected bald areas. In the drug's early days, test studies were conducted to see what side effects, if any, would affect people in a controlled environment. In one study, 2,300 patients with male pattern baldness were given the drug by physicians who gave the real drug to only so many and a placebo (a fake) to the others. The results were as follows: Based on the patient's own evaluation at the end of four months, the drug grew moderate to dense hair in 26% of the patients and the placebo grew moderate to dense hair in 11% of the 2,300 patients. Yes! Approximately 253 patients using a fake solution on their balding or totally bald heads, grew a substantial amount of hair. They didn't know that what they were applying to their heads had absolutely no medication in it. Apparently, some men had such faith and belief in the solution applied to their heads that they grew new hair without any real medicine.

In another study of allergy medication, the results were similar. Of the test study on side effects, 12% of the patients taking the drug complained of headaches as opposed to 11% of the patients taking the placebo. Another 8% taking the drug complained of drowsiness as opposed to 6% who took the placebo and complained of drowsiness. The patients taking the placebo should not have had any complaints.

It is possible that your health, all that happens inside your body, has to do with what your mind believes to be true, even if it is a distortion of reality.

It's always easier to believe than to deny.
Our minds are naturally affirmative.

> *--John Burroughs*
> *Naturalist/Author*
> *(1837-1921)*

8
The Subconscious Mind

Ninety-nine percent of the failures
come from people who have the habit of
making excuses.

> *--George Washington Carver*
> *American Agriculture Chemist/*
> *Educator*
> *(1864-1943)*

The Conscious and Subconscious Mind

You possess both a conscious and subconscious mind. You may wonder how each one functions. I found the best explanation in a book by Dr. Joseph Murphy entitled The Power Of Your Subconscious Mind. He wrote, "The conscious mind is like the navigator or captain at the bridge of a ship. He directs the ship and signals orders to men in the engine room, who in turn control all the boilers, instruments, gauges, etc. The men in the engine room do not know where they are going; they follow orders. They would go on the rocks if the man on the bridge issued faulty or wrong instructions... The men in the engine room obey him because he is in charge..." Likewise, your subconscious mind is like the men in the engine room who accept all the orders (thoughts) as true.

Dr. Murphy also quotes William James, the father of American psychology, who said, "The power to move the world is in your subconscious mind. Your subconscious mind is one with infinite intelligence and boundless wisdom. It is fed by hidden springs and is called the law of life. Whatever you impress upon your subconscious mind, the latter will move heaven and earth to bring it to pass. You must, therefore, impress it with right ideas and constructive thoughts."

Think of the subconscious mind as an energy source, similar to a lighthouse sending light out into the night. The subconscious flashes thought impulses automatically without effort into the conscious mind. Your conscious mind, the reality orientation part of your mind, receives these thoughts twenty-four hours every day, even while you sleep.

In the literary classic, Of Mice And Men, there are two main characters: One, a very big character, but also very slow in the mind, with the intelligence of a two-year-old, but the strength of a bull, the other character is the smart one. The smart one tells the big guy what to do.

This is the way you should think of your subconscious mind: make believe that your conscious mind, the smart one, has to keep the subconscious mind, the big and powerful one, informed with positive thoughts and actions, and that the subconscious mind is strong enough to move all the obstacles out of the way for the smaller, conscious mind.

The danger lies in the fact that, if given the wrong set of instructions, the bigger subconscious mind can ruin your thinking by sending negative impulses to the conscious mind.

Thomas Edison invented the phonograph player or, as it was better known in those days, the "Talking Machine." Edison went about inventing this device differently from the way he invented the electric light bulb, which took him more than 10,000 experiments to perfect. He invented the phonograph by mere thought. It popped into his head one day and he immediately wrote down his thoughts, and then made a working copy.

Was it luck? Was it skill? No, it was conditioning. Edison's conscious and subconscious minds had been conditioned to work together.

The human body can be flabby or well toned and muscular. When muscles are out of shape and exercised, they first hurt, while becoming slowly toned. Once in shape they are rigid and taut. Our conscious and subconscious can work together similar to the way well-toned muscles work.

One day I watched as workers cut down a large tree. I was amazed that the tree had started out as a twig and, if stepped on, could have easily been destroyed. But slowly through growth, the tree became stronger and grew to its current six-foot width. I realized how a mind is like that tree. If your mind is not encouraged to grow, you or someone else can stomp out your mental growth and success. If you allow your mind to grow, your conscious and subconscious can be strong allies, helping you to have a rewarding life and bear good fruit.

> *The credit belongs to the man who is*
> *actually in the arena, whose face is marred*
> *by dust and sweat and blood; who strives valiantly;*
> *who errs and comes up short again and again, who*
> *knows the great enthusiasms, the great devotions,*
> *and spends himself in a worthy cause; who at best,*
> *knows the triumph of high achievement; and who, at*
> *the worst, if he fails, at least fails while daring*
> *greatly, so that his place shall never be with*
> *those cold and timid souls who know neither victory*
> nor defeat.

> *--Theodore Roosevelt*
> *26th United States President*
> *(1858-1919)*

Positive Reaffirming

Now let's talk about "Positive Reaffirming," that is, reinforcing your subconscious with positive thoughts.

Remember: the subconscious mind cannot distinguish the truth from a falsehood.

If you tell yourself constantly that you get uncontrollably tired at 9:00 P.M. every night, soon enough you will always become exhausted each night at 9:00 P.M.

To maintain a positive mental attitude, you must continually, consciously, reaffirm that you are a capable, good, valuable, warm, and caring individual who is productive and able to accomplish everything you want to. The starting point to greatness is in loving yourself. You are worthy of greatness. You love yourself. Your subconscious mind must be reminded repeatedly, much as a child is, of how good of a person you are, how you love yourself, and that now is the time to get on with your success. Your subconscious will accept all repetitive signals and messages.

There is a story about an experiment where, under medical supervision, a group of orphan babies were divided into two groups. One group of babies was given plenty of attention and love. They were hugged often. These babies were talked to and the nurses were told to give them all the special attention they could. The second group of babies was fed properly. Their diapers were changed regularly, and all proper medical attention given, but there was no holding, no loving, no talking to, no cuddling, and no special attention.

The experiment was done to find out if, by some chance, giving love and attention made any difference in how a baby was to grow and respond. The group of babies that had the special attention grew normally, had excellent health, smiled more, and showed that everything was going fine.

The second group of babies who were given no special love or attention did not do well at all. They did not grow properly and were below average weight. They became sicker, so much so that the experiment was ordered to be stopped for fear of death to the infants.

The experiment shows how, even at the youngest age, love and positive affirmation are needed for survival. A healthy mind means having a healthy, loving acceptance from others and from yourself.

The more you receive constant, positive, and loving thoughts the more you are willing to succeed.

Small Victories

If you are not working on receiving positive thoughts, negative thoughts may be flowing into your subconscious without your knowing it.

You might be bombarded with negative thoughts just from the news. Experts have said that 96% of all our conversation is negative and that 90% of all the things around us are negative.

It is time for you to filter out some of the junk every day.

You should try for "small victories" of positive thoughts to your subconscious mind. Learn to celebrate your accomplishments, such as completing a difficult task or being successful at something new.

Almost anything can be called a "small victory," which must meet these guidelines: it must be a legitimate accomplishment and it must be believable. If it is legitimate, pass it into your subconscious by praising yourself. A "small victory" can be something as unimportant as doing a chore around the house.

Each "small victory" can be passed on to your subconscious by visualizing your completed task and doing it with a feeling of euphoria. Visualizing the accomplishment will allow the message to be absorbed into your powerful, subconscious mind.

Celebrate your "small victories" every chance you get. These victories become your self-esteem boosters. Learning to see your accomplishments, even in small ways, creates a mental attitude of wanting to accomplish more.

Constantly try to reinforce your subconscious with small victories. Think of your mind as a large pool filled with water, but the pool has a hole or several holes caused by negative thoughts. The positive reaffirming thoughts and "small victories" represent the water filling up the pool, but the pool must be filled on a daily basis. When the pool is full, your whole world will be fine.

Remember to work at filling your mind with positive thoughts because those negative forces that surround you will not stop at trying to influence your mind.

Begin each morning by making your "Things To Do" list. Keep your list to no more than 10 simple items to accomplish in the day, whether they are for business or personal goals. Just 10 things.

Each item does not have to be something phenomenal, but it has to be a legitimate goal.

One item on your list, although it might appear minor, could be learning to give someone a sincere compliment. It must be sincere and it must make the other person feel good. Helping someone to feel good will help you to feel good too. Doing something good for someone always has great rewards.

At the end of the day, it's time to celebrate! Feel happy and excited as you cross out what you have accomplished on the list that day. You deserve to feel great about yourself for your accomplishments. In celebrating your accomplishments, you've convinced your subconscious to think positive thoughts about yourself and encouraged your subconscious to help you with your next goal.

The "Things To Do" list is very important for a few reasons.

The small victories make you feel that you are useful and worthy of accomplishing real goals. Without your "To Do" list and celebrating your accomplishments, you may be taking yourself for granted and not learning to use the conscious and subconscious powers of your mind to the fullest.

Look for the good. Savor the great things. You will see yourself making new accomplishments, and doing what others refuse to do.

The difference between a successful person and others is not a lack of strength, not a lack of knowledge, but rather in a lack of will.

--Vince Lombardi
Football Coach
(1913-1970)

9
Positive Reaffirming

Every problem is an opportunity,
and every person is a possibility.

--Robert Schuller
Author/Clergy

Input of the Good

The subconscious mind is so powerful it must be treated with respect. You now know that you must control the thoughts that you feed your mind because your attitudes can greatly affect your actions.

To go one step further in understanding the mind and how it works, let's consider hypnosis. In <u>Helping</u> <u>Yourself</u> <u>With</u> <u>Self</u> <u>Hypnosis,</u> the authors, Frank S. Caprio, M.D. and Joseph R. Berger explain hypnosis. "Hypnosis may be defined as a sleep-like condition produced by the hypnotist in a subject who allows himself to accept and respond to certain specific suggestions."

Leslie LeCron, psychologist and lecturer on hypnotism, describes hypnosis as "the uncritical acceptance of a suggestion by the patient in a trance." The author further explains, "Hypnotists do not possess any unusual or mystic power. A hypnotist is a person who knows that his subject actually hypnotizes himself. The hypnotist is merely a person who has learned or perhaps mastered the science and art of effective suggestion."

A hypnotized person will do the most amazing and ridiculous things. The person will bark like a dog, snort like a pig, crawl on the floor, and even stand on his head. It's said that a hypnotized person will do everything asked of him, except things he has strong personal convictions against, such as hurting or killing someone.

I believe that when two people stare intently into each other's eyes with love, they are using powers similar to hypnosis. If there is an attraction, that attraction intensifies into a deep feeling of love.

Love, in my estimation, is a process of convincing your subconscious, through constant thought patterns, that you believe you like a person. The subconscious mind, after a certain amount of time, accepts, believes, and relays these same feelings through thought impulses to the conscious mind. Thus, we have the feeling of love. The brain also releases the mixture of chemicals that make us feel better.

It has been proven that humans are capable of talking to themselves at all times through subconscious thinking. This talking can take place at a rate up to 500 words per minute. That's quite a lot of thinking.

Keep 500 words in mind. Are they positive or negative words? The thoughts that go into the subconscious will then impress themselves upon your conscious mind.

Your mind needs to be replenished each day with thoughts of goodness, kindness, and hope for the future. Here's why: From the moment you get up, you are faced with difficult and, sometimes, negative events throughout the day. In the course of the day, there are numerous negative influences that can affect your outlook.

You may have to get up early and rush out the door, only to fight traffic while getting to work. You work all day and fight your way back home in order to cook a meal for your family. When you turn on the television, your mind is being fed mostly negative news of the day. Although the news can occasionally inspire you to help someone who needs help, for the most part, you are absorbing more negativity.

I am not suggesting that you ignore all the news or the world around you. The point is this: Be aware of what you are taking into your mind. You can control how much negativity you allow into your mind. Without better control, you could be like a rowboat in the middle of the ocean, being pushed to and fro by the waves and the winds.

Think of protecting your positive mental attitude the same way you would protect the finish of a car against the negative elements of the weather, as well as the salt and dirt along the road. By maintaining the finish with a good wax, the car's paint will remain in the best condition over many years. By feeding the mind positive ideas, those positive ideas protect the mind from the impact of negative ideas, attitudes, and experiences. You can control your mind with positive, self-affirming thoughts. You can reassure yourself by saying, "That's all right!" If you make a mistake, that's all right. You can correct the mistake and go on.

Orison S. Marden, Founder of Success Magazine, said, "Our destiny changes with our thought; we shall become what we wish to become, do what we wish to do, when our habitual thought corresponds with our desire."

Exercise your mind by reading positive books regularly. Don't let your mind stagnate. Think creatively, take risks, and act on what you want. Only then will your life become greater!

Positive Self-Suggestion

Each night before dozing off to sleep, think about the 10 best things going on in your life. They must be genuine, not imagined, and they must be very good things.

With regard to looking for good in all people, Napoleon Hill said, "Dig for the gold, the good, sometimes you have to move tons of dirt to find the gold."

The good things in your life could be any number of hundreds of things: a new car, a spouse that makes you happy, a fantastic acquaintance, or a new job that gives you a great sense of accomplishment. Think about what makes these things so special. Dwell on all of them. It's important that your mind accepts those happy thoughts right before you fall off to sleep. These happy thoughts allow your subconscious to give you a positive, life-affirming outlook that, in turn, feed these impulses to your conscious mind.

With ordinary talent and extraordinary perseverance all things are attainable.

--Buckston
Philosopher

In the Audio Program "Insight" by Nightingale Conant, Napoleon Hill, author of <u>Think</u> <u>and</u> <u>Grow</u> <u>Rich</u>, said: "One of the queer things about mankind consists in the fact that the vast majority of people are born, grow up, struggle, go through life in misery and in failure, never getting out of life what they want, not recognizing that it would be just as easy, by a turn of the hand, so to speak, to switch over and get out of life exactly what they want, not recognizing that the mind attracts the thing that the mind dwells upon. You can think about poverty, you can think about failure, you can think about defeat, and that's exactly what you'll get.

You can think about success, you can think about opulence, you can think achievement, and that's what you'll get."

"Positive self-suggestion", as I call it, means feeding the subconscious positive suggestions repeatedly and in a sequence that you're used to. In addition, certain bad habits can be permanently eliminated through this method.

Athletes practice and exercise their bodies in a regimen that is designed to maximize their results in a given sport. Because of their intense preparation, their subconscious mind convince their conscious mind that they can in fact perform better than their competitors.

A person can convince himself to make one of two outcomes: he will win through self-suggestion or fail through self-doubt, even though he is well prepared. An athlete has to believe beyond doubt that he can win in order to win. Self-doubt will cause anyone to lose in every endeavor he wants to do.

The sports underdog has on occasion beaten the highly favored athlete because the underdog came to possess greater positive self-suggestive thoughts. It's known that "trash talking," that is, telling your opponent he is no good, is used in some sports in order to defeat the opponent mentally. An athlete must maintain enough self-confidence to deflect any negativity thrown at him by his opponent.

Over the years I have personally formulated a set of "Positive Self-Suggestion" statements that I repeat to myself every single morning while shaving and also repeat at random times throughout the day. It's very important to keep the statements in the exact same format and content for at least 20 days (Remember that it takes a full 20-day period for a new habit to form).

It's also important to say the positive statements of reassurance every time something good, or even slightly good, happens to you. You can say your "Positive Self-Suggestion" statements at various times: after showering, after your workday is over, after you get your paycheck, after a good meal, or during an exercise workout.

I also repeat the statements during short walks or right before I meet a client. Your subconscious mind accepts the positive statements readily at the times when your conscious mind is feeling happy and good. These statements, though, can be said at any time.

You should customize your own statements to fit your own personality and needs, but always say the positive statements about yourself with plenty of feeling! As an example, here are my "Positive Self-suggestion" statements that have helped to improve my life:

<u>My Positive Self-Suggestion Statements</u>

"I feel healthy; I feel happy; I feel terrific!

I like myself! I like myself! I like myself!

I will be successful; it's inevitable because my aggressiveness will equal opportunities for my success!

I can, I will, I want to!

All things are possible through belief in myself and the Lord, and with His help I can accomplish anything!

I feel great! I feel wonderful, I've got the world by the tail!

If I start acting enthusiastic, I will become enthusiastic!

If I start acting positive, I will become positive!

If I start acting happy, I will become happy!

It's amazing: when I act enthusiastic, others around me become enthusiastic!

It's amazing: when I act positive, others around me become positive!

It's amazing: when I act happy, others around me become happy!

We've got choices in life; we can act enthusiastic or we can act blasé. I choose to act enthusiastic!

We can act positive or we can act negative. I choose to act positive.

We can act happy or we can act sad. I choose to act happy. Why would anyone in his right mind want to act sad?

The Lord is my Shepherd-I shall not fear!

The Lord is my Shepherd-I shall not fear!

The Lord is my Shepherd, I shall not Fear!

You know, I really do feel healthy! I really do feel happy!

I really do feel terrific!

I have a wonderful loving wife who will love me to the day I die.

I have a fabulous job that pays me extremely well, yet challenges me every single day.

I have a brand new luxury car every few years that will take me anywhere I want to go and any time I want to go.

I have enough money saved up that I can to stop working for the next 4, 5, 6, or 7 years. I can even take up singing, painting or writing and still be able to survive.

I really do have it made. I really do have the world by the tail, and I thank God every day."

These statements and thoughts become part of my daily ritual. It keeps me as positive as I possibly can be. I can modify the content of the statements at any time, but I have kept everything basically the same for more than twenty years.

Of all these statements, the one powerful statement I say by itself whenever I need a little extra self-help is, "The Lord is my Shepherd, I shall not fear!"

Just use this statement anytime you feel scared or unsure. Say the statement a few times with emotion and in a believable tone. A certain sense of peace will fill you, almost as if you can do anything and nothing can hurt you. You will actually feel the stress being released from your body.

"Positive self-suggestion" statements will improve your thinking and your life.

Everyone has his superstitions. One
of mine has always been when I started
to go anywhere, or to do anything, never
to turn back or to stop until the thing
intended was accomplished.

> *--Ulysses S. Grant*
> *18th United States President*
> *(1822-1885)*

10
Perseverance: A Trait To Learn

Never give in, Never, Never, Never, Never in nothing great or small - Never give in except to convictions of honor and good sense.

> *--Winston Churchill*
> *Statesman*
> *(1874-1965)*

Persistence Can Be An Inspiration

A baseball game is a contest that runs at least nine innings. Football games run at least four quarters, and basketball games run forty-eight minutes. Your do not start out life as an instant success. It may take years before you see any benefits from your actions. The important thing is to never give up in seeking to achieve your goals.

A great example of perseverance is when an author sets out to write a book. Writing a book can be a labor of love. In my writing experience, it has taken me more than four years to finish writing a book. Many times during those four years tremendous feelings of doubt set in testing my will to push on. The only way I could deal with the self-doubts in order to complete the book was with positive self-statements. Writing a book for four years is a very lonely journey. One must fight off all the obstacles of failure that arise.

Is perseverance important? You bet. I discovered that I could treat each chapter as a small victory, which built up my self-confidence. Once you develop a burning desire to fulfill a goal and accomplish a task, you will be well on your way to achieving that goal. It's as if you become internally deaf to the negative impulses that are communicated to you along the way.

I am motivated by wanting to make a substantial difference in this world before my working days are over. I want to be able to look back on a full and successful career. I would like to leave a positive mark on my world. This is the motivation. This is my burning desire.

Stay aware of the passage of time. Time waits for no one. All the money in the world will never be able to freeze the clock. It will keep ticking away.

Just think about yourself five years ago. What were you doing? What job duties were you performing? Does it seem like five full years have passed? Over 1,800 days are gone forever.

A person who knows the importance of the lapse of time will be a person who accomplishes more in life. That person does not want to be a sleeper or an average person. Become a leader whom others seek to follow. There's no greater honor than to be followed by others who admire your spirit.

Many people stop forging ahead with their careers because they are coasting along until retirement. Other people have given up on their momentum just when they were about to become successful or were near to accomplishing a great goal. Why do some people seem to never stop and never be satisfied, while others stop making improvements?

Psychologists tell us that some people are actually frightened by the thought of success. They're scared of what success will bring or they feel that they just don't deserve to be successful. Others may stop pursuing greater success because they've reached their comfort level Therefore, they stop pushing themselves. And it is a push! Success can be a struggle that requires a strong desire and an intense will to succeed.

Success does not come and grab you. You must go out and grab it.

Remember, the positive self-suggestion: "I will be successful; it's inevitable because my aggressiveness will create new opportunities for my success." Make this your motto. Repeat your own self-suggestion statements to yourself daily. Write them down.

I will persist until I succeed.
I was not delivered into this world in
defeat, nor does failure course in my veins.
I am not a sheep waiting to be prodded by my
shepherd. I am a lion and I refuse to talk, to

walk, to sleep with the sheep. I will hear
not those who weep and complain, for their
disease is contagious. Let them join the sheep.
The slaughterhouse of failure is not my destiny.
I will persist until I succeed.

--Og Mandino
Motivational Author
(1923-1996)

You were not born successful. You were born with abilities, traits, and a degree of intelligence that can be combined to make you successful and those things will help you to accomplish great goals. Successful people have learned to work hard, to seek out new opportunities, and to take risks along the way.

The best example of this is the following record of an individual:

At age 22 he failed in business.

At age 23 he ran for State Legislature and was defeated.

At age 24 he failed once more in business.

At age 25 he was elected to the State Legislature.

At age 26 his sweetheart died at an early age.

At age 27 he had a nervous breakdown.

At age 29 he was defeated for Speaker.

At age 31 he was defeated for Elector.

At age 34 he was defeated for Congress.

At age 37 he was elected to Congress.

At age 39 he was defeated for Congress.

At age 46 he was defeated for Senate.

At age 47 he was defeated for Vice President.

At age 49 he was defeated for Senate.

At age 51 he was elected the 16th President of the United States.

--Author Unknown

This great man, of course, was Abraham Lincoln, the 16th President of the United States. Thank goodness Lincoln was not a quitter. If he had been a quitter, the country would have missed out on having one of its greatest presidents.

To paraphrase the words of Jesus, "Nothing will be impossible to you if you have faith the size of a mustard seed." (Matthew 17:20)

Conrad Hilton said, "Success seems to be connected with action. Successful men keep moving. They make mistakes, but they don't quit."

Because success can sometimes take a very long time, that doesn't mean you should stop trying. Try not to let yourself become discouraged. Everyone fails from time to time. The Beatles were turned down for a record contract by Decca Records which didn't like their sound. Reggie Jackson, the great Hall Of Fame baseball player, struck out 2,597 times in 21 seasons with four teams. A strike out is a failure to hit the baseball. Yet all those strikeouts didn't keep him out of the Hall of Fame. He was inducted into the baseball's Hall of Fame in 1993, baseball's highest honor and was on the All Star team 14 times.

Maybe another player would have changed his swing or taken more pitches or played more carefully, but not Reggie. He just kept on swinging, and swinging hard. He was nicknamed "Mr.

October" because near the end of the season when it counted the most, he did amazing things. Reggie wound up with 2,584 hits, of which 563 were Home Runs.

Even Robert Fulton, the inventor of the steamship, was ridiculed and thought to be a fool by the people of his day.

This excerpt appeared in Insight: "Here's an extract from a notebook of Robert Fulton, who invented the steamship, who changed ships forever from sail to steam on the oceans of the world. He wrote, 'As I had the occasion daily to pass to and from the shipyard where my boat was in progress, I often loitered near the groups of strangers and heard various remarks as to the object of the new vehicle. The language was uniformly that of scorn, sneer or ridicule. The loud laugh often rose at my expense; the dry jest; the wise calculations of losses or expenditures; the dull repetition of "Fulton's Folly." Never did a single encouraging remark, a bright hope, a warm wish cross my path.'"

Emerson said, "To be great is to be misunderstood."

Do you really think it was easier to excel a hundred or two hundred years ago or that people were easier to get along with? I don't think so, not after reading Fulton's notes. I don't think it's ever been easy to succeed. We have some inventions that make our lives easier today now that we have the computer, cell phones, Internet, and other technological advances.

Although the technology is better today, you may still have to work hard to succeed and to accomplish a great goal.

Henry Ford, the pioneer of the Model T Ford, wanted his engineers to build an eight-cylinder engine, a V-8 engine. After studying the proposal, they thought it couldn't be done. Ford told them to forget about the fact that it couldn't be built and get to work until it was done.

After six months, the engineers came back to Ford and told him they couldn't do it. Ford told them to continue no matter how long it took, but do it. After six more months, they still could not build this engine and told Henry Ford that it was impossible. Ford ignored the word "impossible" and told them to get back to work on the eight cylinder engine and don't stop until they've got it working.

The engineers did as they were told and came back with a phenomenal V-8 engine that made some of the Ford automobiles the hottest cars of the time. The V-8 is still in use today.

Ford could have given up because experts in the field told him repeatedly his idea was impossible, yet Ford believed his idea was possible. He knew it wouldn't be easy, yet he repeatedly told them during their failures "I want it and I'll have it."

Great works are performed not by strength but by perseverance. He that shall walk with vigor, three hours a day will pass, in seven years, a space equal to the circumference of the globe.

--Samuel Johnson
English lexicographer/Author
(1709-1784)

Tom Peters, in his book <u>In</u> <u>Search</u> <u>of</u> <u>Excellence,</u> gives another example of successful thinking and aggressiveness to make things happen. He tells the story of Lee Iacocca in the 1970s when he was the CEO of Chrysler: "Lee Iacocca got it into his head that he wanted a convertible; he thought it was a good idea. So he did exactly what you're supposed to do when you have an idea like that. He went to the chief engineer of the Chrysler Corporation and said, 'I'd like to get a convertible developed.'

"The head engineer said exactly what you would expect the head engineer to say to the chairman of the board. First he said, 'Yes sir.' The next words out of his mouth, consistent with conventional wisdom, were, 'We can have one for you in just about nine months.'

"Iacocca turned slightly purple with rage, turned to the chief engineer and said, 'No! You do not understand! Take a car and saw the top off the damn thing!'

"And saw the top off the damn thing they did. Then Iacocca conducted some very systematic and substantial market research. In his new convertible car, he drove around the city of Detroit and counted the people who waved to him. When the number of waves got high enough, he said to his people, 'Build it.' And along with the K-car, the convertible has perhaps been the most successful

Chrysler product during the Iacocca reign."

There's a man who knows how to be different.

*Failure is the opportunity to begin
again more intelligently.*

*--Henry Ford
Inventor/Automobile Manufacturer
(1863-1947)*

The Success Attitude

Here's another visionary. At age 65, this particular man was practically flat broke. He had sold his small restaurant business a few years earlier. That money and his pension money were not enough. He took the one thing he had left, his knowledge, and took to the road to show his recipe and method of cooking to other restaurants. After just a few years at the age of 68, this man started the now famous Kentucky Fried Chicken franchise which is still thriving in many states and countries across the globe.

At a time when most people slow down in their lives, Colonel Sanders used necessity, survival, and pure will to attain success. It simply took him 67 years to attain his greater success.

There are times when a failure will trigger an aggressive reaction in people, somewhat like a fighter who has his back to the ropes and then, all of a sudden with a burst of energy and adrenaline, he charges forward fighting harder than before.

We've all experienced failures of some kind. You know the times when you've reacted aggressively not to let a failure stop you. You need to use your positive aggressive reflexes that you use towards failures to make your life better and accomplish your greatness in life. It may take a little more to convince yourself through positive self-talk to your subconscious that you are good and you can accomplish great achievements. In this way, successful surges will burst into your consciousness when you face any difficulty. Don't underestimate the power of your mind. Successful people are successful thinkers.

Failures will happen, but winners see success as inevitable; it's just a question of how long it will take. That's the best attitude to have. I know of a sweatshirt that read, "I Have An Attitude." We should all wear a sweatshirt that instead reads: "I Have A Success Attitude."

Keep working on your success attitude all day long.

Many people read self-help books and do nothing. Don't just read a book. Study it. Absorb it. Make notes. Write down what changes you plan to make in your life and how you will change. Remember also that a doctor does not become qualified to heal in two years. What makes anyone think that a "Success Degree" takes any less effort? Study; write; memorize; it's all part of the price you pay to achieve your greatest goals that lie ahead of you. Most people won't pay the price it takes to succeed. Will you?

Feed a tree. Water it, fertilize it, keep it where there's sun, and your tree will bear fruit. Deprive the tree and it dies. Deprive your mind of new ideas and positive reinforcing statements and you'll be much like a robot stuck in a rut.

Besides this book, I have written four novels. I believe that everyone has at least one good book waiting to be written. The trouble with writing that book is that most people can't put their lives on hold to write. <u>Better</u> <u>Off</u> <u>Dead</u> took me a total seven years to complete while I juggled work, family, and other responsibilities.

Successful writers are usually consumed with the project until its completion. They may put writing aside for days or even a week, but they never give up. They never stop thinking about the finish line. There's a tremendous sense of accomplishment in finishing a book. Some writers may have a sense of fighting all the way with the ideas till the book is finally finished.

Some people may believe that you need a special gift to be able to write a book. I don't agree. I believe the difference is that successful writers don't give in to defeatist thinking.

Whatever you wish to accomplish, you can. "If you think and see it done, you can complete it." It's positive visualization. Maybe it's not a book, maybe it's restoring an antique car or remodeling a home. Just visualize the project in its completed state and never ever lose that picture. Be <u>consumed</u> until the project is complete. And if you have doubts and problems along the way, as you likely will, keep focusing on the finished project and let your subconscious mind provide you with new ideas that solve the problems as they come.

To be different means you are willing to work hard at accomplishing a great task for as long as it takes without giving up. Over the past 30 years I have come to the realization that the people that are totally consumed with "their goal," whatever it may be, will find a way to achieve that goal.

He has achieved success who
has worked well, laughed often
and loved much.

--Elbert Hubbard
Author/Publisher
(1856-1915)

11
Positive Visualization

Few will have the greatness to bend
history itself; but each of us can work
to change a small portion of events, and
in the total of all those acts will be
written the history of this generation.

--Robert F. Kennedy
Politician
(1925-1968)

A Mental Picture

Positive Visualization is the visualization before beginning a chosen task. It's knowing one-hundred percent that what you are about to undertake can and will be successfully completed, and the picture of the completion is crystal clear in your mind.

Positive visualization is also confidence, the confidence that you *can,* you know how, and you *will* accomplish your goal. All of this happens in a split second, many times, and takes place in your subconscious, which sends out signals to your conscious mind. An artist sketching a picture by hand of a future painting is a perfect example of positive visualization.

I have used positive visualization many times. I've used it when planning a woodworking project such as making a coffee table or an oak porch swing. In my mind, I planned out the end result and how I could accomplish it. The confidence created by positive visualization is tremendous. Once set in my mind, I would meticulously work unaffected by any negativity, until the successful picture in my mind was accomplished in exacting detail.

Positive visualization works in all occupations. In life insurance sales, the agent writes down a prospective client's name, visualizes the person, his needs, and visualizes the appropriate products he would sell to satisfy the prospect's needs.

The salesperson had his mind conditioned with the positive visualization. He knew that the client was going to buy. His attitude was not "can I see you?" but rather "since you're going to see me and buy anyway, which day would be more convenient for you, Tuesday or Thursday?"

Positive visualization is the same thing that happens every time you go into auto-pilot and do a task automatically. Your mind is focusing on positive visualization.

Positive visualization happens when you put the key in the ignition of your car. You remember how to drive the car. Every time you parallel park, you know you can do it. When you ride a bicycle, your mind remembers what to do. Positive visualization happens when your subconscious mind remembers how to do things without thinking about every small step. All you have to do is use this same concept in other parts of your life.

While you can use your mind for positive visualization to capitalize on excelling to meet your goals, you, also, can use your mind incorrectly, resulting in negative consequences.

Do not go where the path may lead,
go instead where there is no path and
leave a trail.

> *--Ralph Waldo Emerson*
> *Essayist/Poet*
> *(1803-1882)*

One night my wife and I went to the Meadowlands racetrack for a night of horse racing. Although I enjoy the racetrack, I very rarely win. This night, however, was different. We hit a triple on the last race and walked away winners. We won approximately $250. Feeling good about winning, I gave my wife some of the winnings to buy something. She had been interested in new shoes.

The next afternoon, a Sunday, we stopped at the local shopping center and my wife bought two pairs of shoes. As we exited the store, we couldn't find our car. We knew we had parked right outside the store.

The shock hit us hard when we realized that our car had been stolen. In the five minutes of shopping, someone stole it. My wife had gained two new pairs of shoes, but we had lost one of our main possessions, our car.

We stood in the parking lot feeling violated and depressed. We waited while the police took our report. Fourteen hours earlier we had a feeling of jubilation, but now we felt depression and anger. Why? What had happened in our minds? What impulses were sent from our subconscious mind? While I felt depression and anger, negative impulses from my subconscious mind were being released on a nonstop basis to my conscious mind.

Think of the negative impulses as a water sprinkler. The sprinkler is the subconscious mind and the water spray is the impulse released from the subconscious. Thousands of drops shoot out nonstop. You have to stop giving yourself negative impulses. Picture all those impulses, but picture them as *positive* impulses. If you condition your subconscious mind to send out positive thoughts, your life automatically will improve.

What would happen if, all of a sudden, with the car stolen, I received a telephone call that I had won a brand new $50,000 Mercedes from an Atlantic City raffle? What would my feelings be at that moment? What impulses would be released at that precise moment from my subconscious mind to my conscious mind? Is it possible that such negative feelings and impulses from the subconscious could be reversed to positive feelings so quickly? Absolutely.

Positive thoughts switch to negative, and negative thoughts can switch to positive thoughts instantaneously, depending on your experiences at the moment.

Think More Positively

It is possible to _fool_ your subconscious into believing that you have something very good happening.

The mind is constantly weighing the good against the bad. When your thoughts dwell upon your problems, your mind seems to forget the good things.

Since the subconscious cannot distinguish between fact and fiction, it will believe what it is fed for the most part. By dwelling on the good things in your life, you can convince your subconscious mind that all is great and wonderful. If you think hard enough, you can come up with a tremendous number of good things about your life. By feeding these positive thoughts into your mind, you can reduce the number of negative thoughts. If you practice for thirty minutes daily, the positive thoughts will be accepted by your mind, which will then release only positive impulses. Exercising the mind with positive thoughts is similar to an aerobics workout for the mind. That's a great mental survival tactic for you to follow.

Positive visualization can be long-term. When you visualize having a successful career so vividly in your mind and the dream becomes so consuming, your mind cannot help but fulfill the dream. This is what happens in many people's rags-to-riches stories.

Remember, you don't have to be very intelligent to become successful. You don't have to be wealthy when you start working on your dream because your intense personal drive to win will help you find the resources you need.

Many people, considered by others to be losers who wouldn't amount to anything, have turned out to be some of the most successful people in the world. One such person was George Herman Ruth, known popularly as Babe Ruth, who became a great Hall of Fame baseball player. Mr. "Home Run" Ruth hit more home runs than anybody had previously done in baseball. While the average number of home runs hit in a season remained around 10-20, Ruth started hitting 30 to 40.

Most important though is how Ruth got started in baseball. Born in 1895 and one of eight children, he hung out as a youngster at the piers in Baltimore. He once described himself in this way, "I was a bum when I was a kid." His family ran a bar in which little George spent much of his time. As a youngster, Ruth turned out to be a wild boy and was labeled "incorrigible" by his school. Totally frustrated, school officials and Ruth's parents agreed that the best place for young Ruth was at St. Mary's Industrial School in Baltimore, a boarding school run by strict Catholic brothers, that received many court-committed children.

The boarding school turned out to be a blessing. It was there that Ruth learned how to play baseball from the brothers. One brother was particularly good at hitting the ball great distances. Ruth looked up to and wanted to emulate that brother the most.

Ruth became unstoppable, first starting out in the major leagues as a pitcher, then later as a fielder. The "Bambino," as he was called, was in the major leagues from 1914 to 1935. In 1927, he set a major league record by hitting 60 home runs. The Babe wound up with 714 career home runs and 2,217 runs batted in.

This one-time "incorrigible" young boy ultimately became inducted into the National Baseball Hall of Fame in 1936. Not bad for someone who was destined to be a bum his whole life. Ruth had developed a tremendous desire to be a long ball hitter. Once he channeled his energy and subconscious mind in the right direction, he could not be stopped.

It has been reported that a single baseball signed by the great Babe Ruth, sells for anywhere between $9,000 and $16,000.

"When it's all over, when all is said and done, what impact will my life have had on this world?" This is a question you should periodically ask yourself. Ruth gained the whole nation's respect and is immortalized to this day in books, films, and articles.

It was the great psychologist and philosopher, William James, who said, "Sow an action and you reap a habit; sow a habit and you reap a character; sow a character and you reap a destiny."

Knowledge is A Steppingstone to Success

Someone once said, "Knowledge is Power." I would like to add: "Knowledge in a given field leads to confidence which leads to success and power."

You do not have to be the most intelligent person. If you do one thing extremely well instead of many things only fairly well, then you have a great chance to go straight to the top in your field.

Earl Nightingale said, "Read all you can - put your hands on about your chosen field, learn all you can about this field." There is always so much more to be learned about a chosen field or about your chosen goal.

I know nothing about the masonry field or working with bricks and concrete. However, I am positive that I could become an expert in five to seven years, but it would take hard work and a lot of focus to learn all I could. By focusing on one field, you could become an expert in almost anything. There's a certain comfort in this thought: you could become an expert in a new field, with proper training, work experience, and hard work to learn all that you need to learn. With your positive energy, focus, and an undying commitment to get to the top of a chosen field, you will be successful.

My dentist, who is an excellent dentist, would probably not be a good plumber if he started that trade tomorrow. He could ultimately excel as a plumber, with the right training, acquired knowledge and positive attitude. Thus, knowledge is very important to building your confidence level. This is why continual learning is essential in order to grow in your field.

Whom do you know in your line of work who studies ten hours a week in order to expand his knowledge and learn more in his chosen field? I don't think you will find too many. But the person who is motivated to study and to learn will excel beyond the average person.

The vast majority of people are JUST AVERAGE. You can choose to be different in order to have more of the knowledge needed to excel.

The average person puts only
25% of his energy and ability into
his work. The world takes off its
hat to those who put in more than 50%
of their capacity, and stands on its
head for those few and far between
souls who devote 100%.

> *--Andrew Carnegie*
> *Industrialist/Humanitarian*
> *(1835-1919)*

12
Your Mind As A Filter?

It's one of the most beautiful
compensations of this life that
no man can sincerely try to help
another without helping himself.

> *--Ralph Waldo Emerson*
> *Essayist/Poet*
> *(1803-1882)*

Filtering Your Thoughts Can Help You

Sometimes people filter out all the wonderful things they have going for themselves and dwell upon all the negative things that surround them everyday. Some people live as if their minds were like a blackboard, choosing to wipe away and forget all the positive things that they should be so happy about. They fill up their blackboards with all the negatives that they are exposed to.

Imagine having only negative thoughts bouncing around all day in your mind. Problems will arise each and every day, but dwelling on the negative experiences or events for long periods of time is unhealthy.

From this day forward, make it a point to begin to filter out the bad thoughts. By filtering out all the doubts, imagine how many great and positive thoughts will be left in your mind.

Filtering represents how you interpret the things that are happening to you.

Filtering is an exercise of your mind. If you allow the muscles in your body to get flabby, you will lose your strength. The muscles are still there, but just less useful. Your mind can work much the same way. You need strong and positive mental activity. If you just "go with the flow," that attitude only makes you as average as everyone else in that crowd.

Reading is an excellent mental activity, as long as you are reading about positive, mind-improvement ideas. "You've got to accentuate the positive, eliminate the negative," as the song goes, from the 1940s.

If we were each promised a sum of five million dollars to put down on paper our own principles for a success formula, I think most people would come up with basic principles that we could all agree on.

What would this experiment show us? Our list would show that you already know within you what you should be doing to find a higher level of success. The challenge is to apply some of this basic knowledge and these attitudes in your life right now. You can constantly fail yourself if you are not applying positive techniques to help you reach new goals and to become better.

Remember to keep life and its setbacks in perspective!

Joel Weldon wrote the following article in Insight regarding gloominess:

"Here is something that appeared in Harper's Weekly:

'It's a gloomy moment in the history of our country.

Not in the lifetime of most men has there been so much grave and deep apprehension.

The domestic economic situation is in chaos. The dollar is weak around the world. Prices are so high as to be utterly impossible.

The political caldron seethes and bubbles with uncertainty. Russia hangs as usual like a cloud - dark and silent upon the horizon. It's a solemn moment. Of our troubles, no man can see the end.'

Does that sound familiar? Well, that article was written in October 1857, just four years before the Civil War. There were poor crops, bank closures, social problems, business failures and government debts."

There will always be negative situations, events, and attitudes surrounding you. The world and the people in it are not perfect. Negatives can become "good" or "useful," if those negatives motivate you to change your negatives into positive results and to accomplish something great.

Negativity always has to be kept in proper prospective. Learning to overcome life's problems and setbacks will help you to reach a new greatness. Strive to be different and greater than your setbacks.

Does the average person give in to defeat and negativity? How can you be different? How can you be successful? Start by minimizing the attention you give to worrying.

There's a great saying: "Don't sweat the small stuff, and it's all small stuff."

Abundance of Opportunities

Consider, too, how times have improved over the centuries. If you lived in the 1700s, it might take you three days to go 300 miles. It's no wonder that many people grew up living and dying in the same general area where they were born, having seldom traveled.

Ben Franklin was different. At the early age of seventeen, he set out to find a life for himself. He left Boston, his birthplace, and hitched aboard a ship headed to New York, a very rough three-day trip in his day. Unable to secure work, he moved on to Philadelphia, where he started his new life.

Today, you can simply take a jet plane to a warm climate within hours. It's a better life by far than what life was like two or three hundred years ago. Also, what we consider toys today, were unthinkable fifty years ago. Today you can buy your son or daughter a $1,000 computer toy. Some *toy!*

If you wanted to, you could drive a car from New York to beautiful Florida. You have the freedom to travel. Nice country, America, isn't it?

You don't have to ask permission to leave your home. There is no immediate threat of attack from a foreign country; no tanks are in our streets fighting a war. I imagine this is the best time in the history of America when there has been this much freedom and money so easy to come by.

Today is a great time to be alive. You can go or do almost anything you wish. I know people who quit their jobs and take off for months to do whatever they want, while they live off their savings.

You have the freedom and the opportunity to choose to do whatever you wish, at anytime you wish to do it. Few other countries in the world offer you as many opportunities to be great and to excel as America does.

In 1915, you had to be rich to own an automobile. Now, some families have four cars, most of which are fairly new. We have food in such abundance in this country; so much so that obesity is becoming a severe problem. There are fast food restaurants providing meals for only ninety-nine cents. Food is affordable.

With the abundance of opportunities around us, what you do with your life is entirely up to you. Thousands of people are risking their lives to cross the border illegally to have the same opportunities we have.

So many obstacles have been moved out of the way for you. As the Army states, you can "be all that you can be," but you need to acquire an all-consuming "desire" for whatever you want. Your subconscious mind has the power to do the rest to help your conscious mind carry forth its goal.

So, learn to use your mind as a filter in a positive way. All the great inventors have learned to do this. They had to filter out all the negative comments, influences and defeatist attitudes that surround them every day. Edison had to get past the derision of others to perfect the light bulb. He could have chosen to give up on his inventions and be an average person, but would we have the electric light bulb today?

What are you capable of? Will your new accomplishments influence others and maybe the whole world?

*For anything worth having one must
pay the price; and the price is always
work, patience, love, self - sacrifice.*

> *--John Burroughs*
> *Naturalist/Author*
> *(1837-1921)*

13
Happiness – It's All Around You

Those only are happy who have
their minds fixed on some object
other than their own happiness, on
the happiness of others, on the
improvements of mankind, even on
some art or pursuit, followed not
as a means, but as itself, an ideal
end. Aiming thus at something else,
they find happiness by the way.

> *--John Stuart Mill*
> *Economist/Philosopher*
> *(1806-1873)*

Happiness is Available to You

Stop searching and start living!

Many people search for happiness in their lives, in their jobs, and in their love lives. Some people are never happy because they are convinced that they lack something. They search and search, but never seem to believe that they've found happiness.

Happiness is all around you, but you must see it, believe in it, and grab onto it.

Happiness is very much a state of mind. Watching President Reagan's funeral, we were reminded about his positive attitudes and the way he encouraged Americans to feel good about their country and themselves. His sincere personality, strong beliefs, and genuine smile taught Americans they could be happy with their country.

You have two basic choices: to be happy or to be miserable. Whether positive or negative, your outlook is a choice you make daily.

Some skeptics who read these pages may think, "Sure, people who have achieved success have an easy time being happy!"

That may be true for some. But there are very successful and well-do-do people who are downright miserable. They may not come right out and say it, but their actions shout it out to everyone. Look at how many celebrities and sports stars are hooked on alcohol and drugs.

There are many reasons why people are not happy and depend on vices, such as excess food, drugs, and alcohol to make them "feel better." The saying holds true: "money alone doesn't make someone happy." All the comforts that money can bring do not help bring happiness.

I can remember having no money in the bank, having an old car, and having to rent a small apartment for eight years. This is how my wife and I lived in the early years of our marriage. We had to count every penny in order to pay our bills and had nothing left over, but they were some of the happiest years of our life.

Maintaining Happiness May Mean a Little Self-indulgence

A little self-indulgence may be a good thing to help you feel better. Human beings need rewards of all types to feel respect and appreciation. It's normal to reward yourself. Rewards range from personal fulfillment, such as buying new clothes, to spiritual fulfillment, such as helping those in need.

You should also work at something you look forward to doing. When you make arrangements three months in advance for a vacation, your subconscious starts to send out positive thought impulses, even if you're not consciously thinking about your upcoming trip.

When you enter a contest or lottery, you have continual hopeful feelings that you might win. When you know that next week you're going out on the town with your friends for dinner and a show, you are excited. No matter how difficult the week becomes, you can deal with everything much better because your mind convinces and reminds you of the good times ahead.

It's a given fact that every automobile needs maintenance. You cannot run a car for 100,000 miles without servicing it. You need to change the oil, the filters, and rotate the tires. The same maintenance principle applies to your mind and body. If you ignore the care of the car, it will break down and eventually stop running. If you don't keep infusing good and rewarding thoughts and actions in your life, you will develop a very pessimistic and regretful attitude.

Allan K. Chalmers, author and philosopher, said, "The grand essentials of happiness are: Something to do, something to love, and something to hope for."

In Insight, Earl Nightingale said: "Back in 1930 Bertrand Russell wrote a small book entitled The Conquest of Happiness (Liveright Publishing Corporation, 1971). Bertrand Russell was 58 in 1930 when he wrote The Conquest Of Happiness, and in it he wrote: 'Now I enjoy life; I might almost say that with every year that passes, I enjoy it more. This is due partly to having discovered what were the things that I most desired, and having gradually acquired many of these things. Partly is due to having acquired many of these things. Partly is due to having successfully dismissed certain objects of desire, such as the acquisition of indubitable knowledge about something or other, as essentially unattainable. But very largely it is due to a diminishing preoccupation with myself. Gradually, I learned to be indifferent to myself and my deficiencies; I came to center my attention increasing by upon external objects: the state of the world, various branches of knowledge, individuals for whom I felt affection.'"

Negative Attitudes Poison Successful Thinking

Control negative thoughts that may start to form in your mind. As soon as you realize these thoughts, replace them with positive self-suggestions: "I am in control of my thoughts, and I choose to remain positive. I will be successful!" Remember: you are capable of winning, of becoming a champion and excelling.

Consider the offspring of a famous thoroughbred horse. That horse comes from a good blood line. The horse, a descendent of the thoroughbred, just needs the right training, care and diet, and quite possibly this horse will be a racing champion.

Unlike that thoroughbred, you <u>don't</u> need a special bloodline to be successful. In fact, you don't need all your arms, legs, and senses either. As long as you can think, you can excel. You may need a lot more training and preparation, but you can excel at something, even if some of your body parts and senses are missing.

You're worth more than 10 million dollars, which, by the way is what you're capable of earning over your lifetime. But we will do so only if we want it bad enough and we have the determination and the will power to excel.

Remember the story of Milo C. Jones, the farmer paralyzed and bedridden? From his bed, he went on to accomplish more than when he was one-hundred percent healthy. He formed a company that produced a breakfast sausage, the Jones Little Pork Sausages, that are still sold today.

You can do anything. If you really had a desire to fix air conditioners, you could go to night school, learn the trade, and get a job fixing them, and then maybe one day even operate your own air conditioning business.

What is it that you really want? Are you willing to put all your heart and soul into accomplishing that goal? It can and will be yours! There's only one catch. You must want your goal so bad that you never stop thinking about it. Every time your mind drifts, it must refocus right back to your all–important, urgent goal and figure out how you want to achieve that goal. As long as you have an all-consuming desire and vision, that goal can become a reality.

Think again about those runners who enter the 26-mile New York City Marathon. The contestants train all year and have the one goal of finishing the race. Most of these runners never run 26-mile races, but this is the one race they set out to finish.

In my case, I had a goal of writing a book. I knew it would be difficult, but I set a goal for myself to write a book. By the time you read this book, I will have completed five books. Was I consumed by my desire to write a book? You can bet I was!

Simply put, if you want your dream badly enough, then you will design ways and muster the energy to make that dream come true.

Just try to remember the last extraordinary accomplishment you had. Maybe it was building a deck, or painting an entire house, or doing an entire landscaping job. Remember your frame of mind. Nothing stood in your way. You could think of little else and you visualized its completion before you had begun. Every person can do great things.

Some Foreigners Maximize the all American Dream

America has always been called the land of opportunity. Consider how many immigrants come to America today knowing very little English and having limited formal education and, yet, they have become successful. Most have come to America with the right attitudes and the burning desire to make their lives better and to succeed. I believe many come believing they will be very successful, as long as they work very hard.

You can understand why some immigrants are so successful. Their minds are focused on the will to succeed. They do not allow thoughts of failure to enter their minds.

The immigrant is expected to make good and, ultimately, he becomes something of a celebrity by all who know him back home.

Failing to succeed in America for some immigrants is tantamount to disgrace. To succeed is a matter of "Positive Expectation." Some people have great positive visualizations of what they expect to achieve.

The next time you walk into a business establishment and see a foreign business owner, just remember how long and hard he has worked to get that business established. He may have worked harder than an American citizen because he had to overcome tremendous obstacles to come to this country. As you look into his eyes, try to visualize the dream that drove him to work so hard.

America, the land of opportunity, helped an unknown author and a lawyer become one of the most successful and famous authors of our time. His name is John Grisham and his best-selling books include The Firm, The Pelican Brief, A Time to Kill, and The Client.

With nothing more than a pen and paper, a person can write a book about almost anything. It's the least expensive hobby around. In America, a person has an opportunity to become a best-selling author like Grisham and have a book turned into a successful motion picture too.

We are all capable of success, if we want it. It's not right to feel sorry for yourself in this country. Remember when, at age 97, George Burns showed that he could still get on a stage to tell jokes. He made it to age 100. He said he would. In fact he had a booking to perform on stage at age 100. It was almost a promise he had to keep to make it to age 100. Remember, you have opportunities all around you, no matter what your age may be.

Without consciously thinking about it, your heart beats roughly 65 beats per minute. It brings oxygen to every part of your body through many miles of arteries and veins. Your lungs inhale approximately 50 gallons of air a minute automatically without thinking. Your body is like a factory, running on automatic pilot at all times, leaving the rest of your brain free to accomplish great goals in life.

Don't let yourself down. Don't let your family down. Don't let your country down by not living up to your maximum potential. The Army slogan is "Be All That You Can Be!"

Create your own positive slogan that you start out repeating each day. I've used this statement to help me to be more successful: "I will be successful; it's inevitable because my aggressiveness will equal opportunities for my success." For the past 25 years, I have been repeating the same self-suggestion statements throughout the day. Write down your own statements. Keep them simple. Slowly create your own list of positive statements over the next several months. As you follow your own positive statements, your life will improve.

14
The Magic Of Believing

That which we are, and if we are ever
to be any better, now is the time to begin.

--Alfred Lord Tennyson
English Poet
(1809-1892)

What You Believe Is Very Important

The magic of believing will help you gain tremendous rewards.

Let's look at an example of belief. When you have pains in your chest, you may become alarmed. After you make an appointment with your doctor, he will give you a complete examination and tell you to come back in order to go over the test results. On the second visit, the doctor tells you that all the tests come back negative and that there is nothing to be concerned about. He explains that perhaps you were affected by stress and that you should try to relax. If you do not feel better, he suggests that you can come back for another visit.

Having heard the good news that nothing is wrong, you leave the doctor's office suddenly feeling fantastic. Your mind gets rid of all your aches and pains that you thought were real.

Belief in something, including your own health, is very powerful. If you learn how to capitalize on the power of belief, you can alter your life for the good.

What if someone promised to pay you $100,000 in return for following a 10-day plan that was not hazardous in any way, morally acceptable to you, and which was guaranteed to improve your life? Would you agree to follow the plan? You probably would because you wanted the $100,000 reward.

Here's the $100,000 self-improvement plan that I am giving you:

$100,000 Self Improvement Experiment

1- Get up at 6 A.M. each morning and study for one hour in your chosen field.

2- Before leaving home each morning, make a list of the 10 most important things to do for the day. At the end of the day, cross off your accomplished tasks.

Remember that each accomplished task is a small victory and the subconscious mind needs to savor its accomplishments.

3- Three times a day - before leaving home each morning, while traveling, and before going to sleep - repeat your own "Positive Self-Suggestion Statements."

You can use the following statements given earlier as a guide or develop your own personal statements that fit your lifestyle and personality.

Positive Self-Suggestion Statements

I feel healthy; I feel happy; I feel terrific.

I like myself; I like myself; I like myself.

I will be successful; it's inevitable because my aggressiveness will equal opportunities for my success.

I can; I will; I want to. I can; I will; I want to.

All things are possible through belief in myself and the Lord;

and with his help I can accomplish anything.

I feel great; I feel wonderful; I've got the world by the tail.

If I start acting enthusiastic, I'll become enthusiastic.

If I start acting positive, I'll become positive.

If I start acting happy, I'll become happy.

It's amazing; but when I act enthusiastic, others around me become enthusiastic.

It's amazing; when I act positive, others around me become positive.

It's amazing; when I act happy, others around me become happy.

We have choices in life; we can act enthusiastic or we can act blasé;

I choose to act enthusiastic.

We can act positive or negative; I choose to act positive.

We can act happy or sad; I choose to act happy. Why would anyone in their right mind want to act sad?

Yes! I do feel healthy; I do feel happy because I am healthy; I do feel terrific. I really do have the world by the tail.

Each day for the next ten days you must look for the good in every situation. No matter how bad it may be, you must find something good about it. Even if the car runs out of gas, say something like this, "That's good; now I can get some needed exercise!" If it starts raining on you, you could say, "The rain is good. We needed more water for the flowers and birds." No matter what happens, you must find good in it and believe there is good happening around you.

Each night before you go to sleep, you are to read for one hour, but you must also read a self-help book.

I'm sure you can fulfill this 10-day plan, especially if you want to be paid the $100,000. Would you still continue the plan if you knew that the company promising the

$100,000 went bankrupt on the second day that you started on the plan?

Many people would give up. Not because they could not complete the plan, but because they were only motivated by the $100,000 offer. Those are the people who may never be successful because they do not have a personal plan and they are not willing to keep working to improve themselves despite a setback with the $100,000 reward.

Are you willing to be different? Do you dare to try to be different? Are you willing to stand out from the crowd? Are you able to put aside people laughing at you or questioning what you are doing in order to accomplish something great, which they do not see? If people do not see immediate success, are you willing to continue on with your dream?

Ever since you were a child, you have been making choices for your life. Now is the time to chose to be different in order to achieve the greatest success possible in what you want to accomplish.

From Failure To Success

Not every successful person started out that way. Many were failures before they turned their lives around.

Energizing themselves by being dissatisfied has turned more unsuccessful people into tremendous successes.

One such person was a man named Og Mandino. Og had hit rock bottom and came very close to taking his own life.

As a youngster, Og's mother would tell him, "Some day you will be a writer...not just a writer but a great writer!"

Og's mother died before he graduated high school and he felt devastated for years. During World War II, he flew thirty bombardier missions over Germany. After the war ended, he got married, had a child, sold life insurance, and slowly drank himself into alcoholism.

It took ten years before he ruined his marriage, forcing his wife and daughter to leave him, and for him to completely bottom out. With his last ten dollars, he contemplated buying the gun he saw in a pawnshop window. Something stopped him from carrying out the suicide he envisioned. Instead, he wound up in a library that day and tried to find an answer for his life in self-help books, and one in particular: <u>Success Through A Positive Mental Attitude</u>.

Og found something that changed his life in those books. He went on to head the magazine "Success Unlimited" and wrote the world renowned book, <u>The Greatest Salesman In The World</u>. He sold over 25 million copies of his many inspirational titles, which became his way of helping millions of people improve their lives.

Og was clearly inspired to action. Positive Visualization? You bet! The magic of believing is powerful when accepted by the subconscious mind.

15
Preventing Success

Far better is it to dare mighty things,
to win glorious triumphs, even though
checkered by failure, than to take rank
with those poor spirits who neither enjoy
much nor suffer much, because they live
in the gray twilight that knows not
victory nor defeat.

> *--Theodore Roosevelt*
> *26th United States President*
> *(1858-1919)*

Excel By Thinking

People fail at success and other endeavors because, quite simply, they choose not to change themselves, their routines, or the world around them. In other words, nothing changes, which creates a logjam of bad habits and negative thinking. For some, life is judged by standards of comfort, not by the struggle to make a better life for themselves and for others.

Out of 100 average people with the exact same education, only a very few will succeed or accomplish things that stand out from the rest. When people attend their high school reunions, they are sometimes astonished to find out that their average schoolmates with only marginal grades somehow managed to become very successful business owners or very prominent citizens.

Statistics show that only a few out of every 100 people have enough drive and perseverance to succeed. The question is, Are you willing to do more, achieve more and go the extra mile than those who will try less hard?

In addition to doing more than others, you need to document on paper and post pictures around you of what you want so you visualize your goals every day. The visual reinforcement adds greater conscious and subconscious determination to accomplish your goals.

Also, it helps to tell relatives and friends about your goals. Of course, those you talk to need to be supportive and provide helpful advice. If someone is not helpful, you need to avoid that person's negativity.

Remember the time you promised to do something for someone, but you did not want to do it? Nevertheless, you went ahead and did what you promised to do for that person. That's the point. Promises, sometimes, motivate you to go the extra mile and do what you thought you could not do. That is the mindset you need to be telling yourself: "I can do more for myself, even though I'm reluctant to start doing it." You can make your impossibilities possible simply by trying harder every day.

It does not matter if the goal seems difficult or unreachable. Just be precise in your goal and develop a plan for achieving your goals. Spell out your goal, such as, "I plan each morning to walk two miles at 6:00 A.M. so that I can lose 10 pounds in one month. Then I plan on maintaining this weight. I plan on losing the extra weight to improve my health and appearance."

Continue telling close friends and relatives, your supporters, about your new goal. By telling people and posting the goal for open viewing, you will be imprinting the goal and its expected outcome into your subconscious. In return, your subconscious will send new thoughts to your conscious mind to help you fulfill your goal.

Dorothea Brand, author of <u>Wake</u> <u>Up</u> <u>and</u> <u>Live</u>, said, "All that is necessary to break the spell of frustration and inertia is this, act as if it were impossible to fail. That's the talisman, the formula, the right about face that runs us from failure to success."

Some Reasons For Failure

Let's look at the opposite of success - total failure. Total failure can be described as an unwillingness or inability to produce successful results.

Why do some people lose the gumption to push, lose the fire, or the drive to pursue the objective?

One reason people may fail is that they lose their motivation. They can't understand why they have to work so hard at each objective. Maybe they had something go wrong in life, such as a failed love relationship or the death of a loved one. In sales, I've seen very competent salespeople fail by burning out, caused by mental and emotional exhaustion. They lose the spark, the magic, and the excitement of their work.

Discover what will give you your drive and burning desire to accomplish something, until failure is not a word acceptable to your mind. Become the rare person who has consuming goals which motivate you every day and you will not stop until your goals have been achieved.

There are some professional boxers with this all-consuming drive. They are "all heart." They can fight a brutal fight for 15 rounds. They can take punishing blows to the head and body, and still refuse to give up. And although they're dead tired, they stay on their feet, just as the hero did in the movie _Rocky_.

They may have been outclassed by a better fighter and may even be losing the fight on points, but their mind tells them to keep on fighting right to the end. Muhammad Ali was such a fighter: He was all heart.

The New York City Marathon always amazes me when I see some 25,000 runners eager to run 26 miles, something most of the runners never do every day. It's marvelous to see all the different people who run, some of whom are in their eighties. In addition to the professional runners, some are disabled and use wheelchairs. One such wheelchair runner had only his top torso and arms, but he finished. He had the motivation, that burning desire to reach a goal, even though he did not win a prize or money. The motivation of some people pushes us on to achieve bigger and better goals. We all admire courage. We all like heroes and winners.

All the participants in the marathon are driven by a tremendous desire to finish the race and accomplish the phenomenal feat of running twenty-six miles. So intense is the desire to finish the marathon that blisters, sprains, and exhaustion don't cause the runners to give up. Approximately 90% of all the runners cross the finish line, even if they walk across it. It's a personal victory for each finisher of the race.

In the 1994 New York City Marathon, three people had heart attacks, two of whom died. Why did two men die of heart attacks after crossing the finish line and minutes after running nonstop for hours? I believe those runners had reached the point of a "burning desire" to finish at all costs. While suggesting that you need to find new burning desires in your life, I am not suggesting that you push yourself to the point of exhaustion or push yourself right into a heart attack. You have to learn to pace yourself as you work towards your success, but a burning desire will help you complete one goal after another, similar to how a runner takes one step after another in order to cross the finish line.

I believe that, if your mind is not pushed and challenged, it could slowly close down parts of your body, leading to health problems. The mind can control the body. We are each actually feeding our minds thousands of thought impulses per hour. Watch those thoughts because they circulate from your subconscious out to your conscious mind.

W. Clement Stone said, "Do what you're afraid to do. When you run away because you are afraid to do something big, you pass opportunity by."

The idea was stated very nicely in Whitney Houston's song, "One Moment In Time," with the words: "Give me one moment in time, where I'm more than I thought I could be, where all of my dreams are a heartbeat away, and the answers are all up to me." The writer Jack London, wrote something similar:

I would rather be ashes than dust! I would rather that my spark should burn out in a brilliant blaze than it should be stifled by dry rot. I would rather be a superb meteor, every atom of me in magnificent glow, than a sleepy and permanent planet. The proper

function of man is to live, not to exist.
I shall not waste my days in trying to
prolong them. I shall use my time.

--Jack London
American Author
(1876-1916)

Let's discuss wealth. Most people want to become millionaires. It doesn't sound too difficult, does it? Well, here are the statistics, as delivered by the U.S. Census Bureau: As of 2002, there were 2.22 million high net worth individuals. The definition of a high net worth individual is someone with financial assets of at least 1 million dollars, excluding real estate. So, just over two million people in the United States are classified as high net worth. The population of the United States is just over 292 million.

It is clearly very difficult to become a millionaire. But it is far easier than it was years ago. After all, a person earning $50,000 a year will have earned $1 million dollars in twenty years.

If we can't be millionaires, we can each strive to be millionaires in our attitudes and the ways we think. Remember, attitude is a state of mind.

When everything seems to be going against you,
remember that the airplane takes off against
the wind, not with it.

> *--Henry Ford*
> *Inventor/Automobile Manufacturer*
> *(1863-1947)*

16
Understanding Negative Habits

Many men fail because they quit too soon. They
lose faith when the signs are against them.
They do not have the courage to hold on, to keep
fighting in spite of that which seems insurmountable.
If more of us would strike out and attempt the
'impossible', we very soon would find the truth of
that old saw that nothing is impossible.... Abolish
fear and you can accomplish anything you wish.

> *--Dr. C.E. Welch*
> *Owner, Welch's Grape Juice Co.*
> *(1852-1926)*
> *Quoted from Success Magazine, 1922*

John Paul Carinci

Bad Habits Can Change

What exactly is a habit? The 1990 <u>American</u> <u>Heritage</u> <u>Dictionary</u> defines habit as "a pattern of behavior acquired by frequent repetition." Everyone has habits, bad ones and good ones.

One bad habit is biting your nails. Smoking is another bad habit. Americans spend millions of dollars on cigarettes and then they develop bad health from the side effects of cigarettes. Eating to excess can also be a bad habit. Others have the bad habit of using profanity in their everyday speech. Not only does excess profanity offend others, the user reveals his lack of self-control and his poor range of vocabulary. Other bad habits can include rudeness or selfishness.

William James, a Harvard professor once said, "The Hell to be endured hereafter of which theology tells us is no worse than the Hell we make for ourselves in the world by habitually fashioning our characters in the wrong way. If we realize the extent to which we are mere walking bundles of habits, we would give more heed to their formation. We are spinning our own fates, good or evil, never to be undone. Every smallest stroke of virtue or vice leaves its never-so little scar."

Worry can become a very bad habit. An unknown author once said: "It's not what you're eating, but what's eating you!"

On occasion, I've eaten sausage and peppers with plenty of onions and the food never bothered my stomach. Yet, on other occasions, I've eaten light meals that churned up tremendous amounts of acid and heartburn. The problem was not always the food, but what was on my mind or my subconscious. There are times people can be filled with worry and stress without being fully aware of their stress.

Think of worry as similar to the blinking cursor on a computer screen; that is, worry is always sending out negative thought impulses. Your eyes typically blink unconsciously at least ten times per minute. In a similar way, you could be allowing worry to pulsate into your thoughts, while constantly hurting your mind and your health. Worry should be seen as a habit and, like any habit, it can be broken.

What does it take to beat the worry habit? You have to begin to reprogram your thinking with new thought patterns. You do this by finding something you enjoy doing such as painting, gardening, walking, reading, or doing crossword puzzles. Then, commit at least one hour each day to the new, happy task. Do this for a minimum of 20 days because, as we know, a habit takes 20 days to be formed, as it takes the same 20 days to break a bad habit.

I've formed good habits in this manner and I'll share some of mine with you.

At age 21 I started my career in the life insurance business. Then, at age 27, I became the youngest district manager that the insurance company ever had. I decided, as a leader, I had to change some habits, especially the bad habit of cursing.

So, as a manager, I decided to stop my cursing. I employed a positive reinforcement technique. Each time I would think of a curse word, I would say very strongly-as if yelling at myself, "Stop cursing! Stop swearing, Stop cursing! Stop swearing!" Each and every time I even heard anyone use the slightest curse word, I would say to myself, "Stop cursing! Stop swearing! Stop!"

Today, many years later, if I hear the slightest curse word, a bell goes off in my mind and I still tell myself very strongly, "Stop cursing! Stop swearing!"

If I stub my toe hard by accident, I still do not curse. It's reconditioned thinking, a way of controlling my subconscious. I will on occasion say words that I have substituted for the cursing, such as "Ah, beans!" or "weasel!"

Anyone can do this mind-conditioning. Try it now.

I even stopped smoking by using this same system. One day I crushed three packs of cigarettes and never had another one again. Each time I became tempted to smoke a cigarette I would think, "Stop! Stop smoking! It's a terrible habit! Stop!" Every habit can be modified by this method.

Remember, the subconscious mind will accept the corrective statements it receives, but they must be strongly stated in a direct manner and said immediately following the bad habit.

Overeating or worrying can be corrected if you truly want to break the habit by making statements such as, "Stop! Stop eating like this! You're hurting yourself! Stop! Stop eating like this! Substitute healthy food for the bad!"

Only one habit should be corrected for each 20 day period at a time. Even if it's four statements long, the same statements have to be repeated in the same order for the full 20 days. You may, as I have done, find yourself using the statements automatically after 20 days.

Worry should be considered a major health hazard. Your heart rate increases, your blood pressure goes up, your blood vessels constrict, and adrenaline is released by your brain. Your muscles tense up and your blood sugar goes up because your mind thinks your body needs extra strength.

Fear and worry typically go together. There's a self-help statement I use to control my worries. Once again, it's worth repeating this statement. It can calm you as it has very often calmed me: "The Lord is my shepherd; I shall not fear." I repeat the statement several times with confidence, and the fear and pressure are lifted from me.

Stress is a known killer. Every day there are people rushed to hospitals with severe chest pains, but, sometimes, they are suffering stress attacks. Stress attacks can mask themselves to simulate a heart attack. I have had such chest pains when I have pushed myself too much at work. Your doctor should always determine if it is a heart attack. When it comes to stress, you could help yourself by using mind-and-body relaxing techniques when you feel stress. There are times when deep breathing and thinking of a relaxing place, such as being on a warm beach, can take away the dangerous stress and worries that could send you to the hospital. The body has different warning signs to tell you to calm down and to cut back on the worry and stressful overworking. Work is good, but not in excess or to the point that it hurts the body.

Needless Worrying

You can diminish stress by becoming self-aware that 90% of the things you worry about are considered by the experts as needless worry. Needless worrying can consume your life, drain your energy, and weaken your immune system, causing you to get sick more easily.

If I find myself worrying needlessly, I tell myself: "Do I have control over this situation? Can I change the outcome? Then forget about it!" That's right. I tell myself, "Forget about it!" As soon as the words are spoken, a certain feeling of relief sets in. You can also say, "And this too shall pass", (Author unknown).

The realization that the outcome of the situation is out of my control relieves the tension. There is a great statement that puts it all in perspective:

Things We Worry About

Things that never happen: 40%.

Things over and past, that can't be changed: 30%.

Needless worries about our health: 12%.

Petty miscellaneous worries: 10%.

175

Real legitimate worries 8%.
Which leaves 92% of all worry we do
as useless.

--Dr. Walter Cavert

We all have a variety of worries and fears as we go through life: the fear of not marrying the right person; failing in business; the fear of dying; the loss of a loved one; the fear of being poor; and thousands of other fears.

You can control your fears by using these techniques:

1- Put the fear in proper perspective.

2- Analyze the fear. Why are you worrying?

3- What is the worst possible thing that could happen? If the worst possible thing does happen, will you still have your mind? Will you still be alive? How terrible will it really be? In reality, how terribly important is this thing that worries you?

4- Write out the worst possible scenario on paper, then remind yourself that 92% of all worrying is not necessary.

Positive thoughts help you create your success. Negative thoughts create a brick wall that surrounds you and keeps you from seeing what you can achieve.

Andrew Carnegie, the millionaire steel industry leader, had positive thoughts when he said, "Take away my factories and my machines, but let me keep my people and within two years I'll be back in business and as successful as ever."

*Thinking will not overcome
fear, but action will.*

> *--W. Clement Stone*
> *Motivational Author*
> *(1902-2002)*

17
The Magic In Selling

*I didn't know enough to quit; I was a
dreamer who believed in the 'gold at the
foot of the rainbow' promise and continued
in the path where wise ones feared to tread.*

--King Camp Gillette

Inventor

(1855-1932)

Everyone "Sells"

Selling is easy. You've been doing it all your life. Ever since you were young, you have been consistently selling. You've used a sales pitch on your parents to get them to buy you toys or candy. Think about all the selling techniques you used when you wanted your parents to buy you a fast food meal in order to get that important toy that came with the meal.

As a child, think of the times you tried convincing your parents to let you stay up late at night or to stay out a little longer to play before coming in to do your homework. You might have tried telling your mother, "Mom, I don't have much homework tonight. I can finish it in fifteen minutes! Let me stay out a little longer."

Babies cry and whine for their moms to hold them or pay attention to them. This is a form of selling which usually gets the babies what they want.

Each time you were interviewed for a new job you were selling yourself. Your résumé was your package that was meant to convince someone in one or two pages that you deserved a particular job.

You're selling all the time in life and at work. Through your performance and words, you're always trying to show why you should move ahead to that next opportunity and promotion.

In relationships, you are always selling yourself in order to attract a mate. You talk and dress in a certain way to make yourself look attractive to your potential spouse. Your personality becomes part of your overall package. To convince your spouse that you need a new car that's worth $20,000 or that you want something that you have to spend money on, you begin appealing to your spouse about what you want and why you need it, as you try to motivate your spouse into action and agreement.

If you have been selling all these different ways, why are some people afraid to "sell" as a job? The key to selling successfully is to believe whole-heartedly in the product or service and believe one-hundred percent that your client will benefit from having it. A piece of art serves no function in the daily needs of a person, but the person bought it for a couple of reasons. First, the artwork may increase its financial value over the years. Secondly, people may grant the owner more respect for owning that artwork. Thirdly, the art piece may add a sense of beauty or dignity to the room. In selling, you often need to know how to appeal to the buyer. When you try to convince someone of what you want, you know (from experience since childhood) to offer multiple reasons to "sell" (convince) the other person to do what you propose.

Politicians can be considered salespeople because they have to convince the voters they are the right person for a political office.

J. Willard Marriott, Sr. of the Marriott Hotel chain said, "I've never been satisfied with anything we've ever built. I've felt that dissatisfaction is the basis of progress. When we become satisfied in business, we become obsolete."

Why do salespeople and people in general often fail to sell something? It's not because they cannot sell. It has to do with motivation and a lack of understanding as to why people do things.

What was the last item you purchased that cost hundreds of dollars? Perhaps a stereo system, a color TV, or new clothes. Why did you purchase this new product? Most likely for the reason you were dissatisfied. You were dissatisfied with something old. You certainly did not spend your money with the altruistic intention of improving the U.S. economy. You purchased an item because something motivated you to act.

Excerpt From A Speech

The following is an excerpt from a speech I gave many years ago at an insurance convention. I was only twenty-four, successful, and chosen to speak to hundreds of my peers for the first time.

"From the time I was a child, I was never satisfied with just listening to the radio or watching television. I wanted more. I wanted to know why. Why did the radio bring in signals from far away? Why did the television show me a picture of someone many miles away? I was curious. I took apart many radios, TV's and tape recorders, and after breaking a couple of them, I was able to fix almost anything.

"When I became a life insurance agent, I was not content with just selling policies to people. I wanted to know why they were buying and why some weren't buying. I wanted to know what it was I was doing right and what I was doing wrong. After years of reading, studying, listening, observing, and attending educational classes, I finally realized why people buy things in general, and in particular why they buy life insurance from me. *They buy only because I disturb them.* Yes! I disturb them so thoroughly about their present situation that they are motivated to act and act now!

"The biggest mistake life insurance agents and financial planners make is that they want to be liked by their customers. They want to be liked so badly that they avoid telling the customer that his family will be in deep trouble financially if he doesn't protect himself with life insurance.

"Don't get me wrong. It's great to be liked, but salespeople shouldn't substitute being liked with doing the right job for prospective customers.

"So, the key to selling is disturbing. Disturbing to the point of positive action! We have it in our power to convince anyone to do what we want them to do as long as we believe without a doubt that it is in his or her best interest to do it.

"The product is the solution. The salesperson shouldn't present the solution before the need or the _problem_ is shown and understood. "Let's look at this more closely. Take for instance, the vacuum cleaner salesperson. The door-to-door vacuum cleaner salesperson doesn't sell a vacuum cleaner just by knocking on doors. The salesperson first gets in the prospective customer's home on a favorable basis. Then, slowly and carefully, presents the problem to the customer, the problem she never knew she had!

"The salesperson takes dirt, ashes and pet hair, and spreads them on the prospective buyer's carpet. The sales person then gets the customer's own vacuum and vacuums the carpet picking up the mess. Then, the salesperson will ask the customer if the carpet is clean. After the prospect says "yes" the salesperson will suggest that she use the new demonstration vacuum cleaner. When she goes ahead and vacuums over the same area cleaned by her vacuum, she hears dirt being picked up by the much more powerful and efficient machine. Then the salesperson removes a clear vacuum cleaner bag that was empty before they started and shows her the additional dirt and hair that had been deeply embedded in her carpet.

"The salesperson then explains why the *solution* to her *problem* can actually save the prospective customer money. The salesperson tells her that with the new machine she won't have to clean the rugs so often or have to replace the carpet sooner than expected. The salesperson further explains that her present vacuum is just not effective and doesn't do the proper job.

"Through this whole process, the salesperson doesn't mention the cost of the new machine. Not until the prospective customer is thoroughly disturbed to the point of acting does the salesperson show how affordable and simple it is for the prospect to purchase the machine. Only at this precise point in the sales process can she rationalize why she must have this new item. Cost becomes incidental at this moment. This process happens in almost all sales situations. It's almost a magical moment when done properly.

"It's amazing, but the salesperson's idea becomes the prospective customer's idea so successfully that she is convinced that she always wanted the item she's buying anyway, when in fact she didn't think about having a problem or needing a solution before the salesperson's presentation.

"Let's look at why the salesperson should <u>DISTURB</u> someone in order to sell. Salespeople know why the prospective customer needs this product. They know their product may be the best solution to the problem. But, remember, the customer doesn't know she has a problem. The salesperson suggests a disturbing problem and that his solution is perfect.

"It's not the prospect's job to know how much life insurance he needs or to know that he is underinsured. It is the salesperson's job to sell, disturb, and convince the prospective customer what he needs.

"It's up to the life insurance sales professionals and other salespeople to disturb, to move, and to provide a good reason why the prospective customer should do something and do it now. Remember: <u>disturb</u> someone to the point that he must take action. Immediate action. Keep this idea in mind when trying to motivate someone to act on something. I know it works and it'll work for you.

"Be enthusiastic. Enthusiasm is contagious. Be proud of what you're doing - you should be. But never, never, be satisfied!"

It's a reality of life that men are competitive,
and the most competitive games draw the most
competitive men. That's why they are there, to
compete, and to win. They know the rules and the
objective of the game, and the objective is to
win, fairly, squarely, decently, but to win, and
in truth I've never known a man worth his salt,
who deep down in the long run didn't appreciate
the grind and discipline. There is something in
good men that yearns for and needs discipline
and the harsh reality of head to head combat. I
don't say these things because I believe in the
brute nature of man, or that man must be
brutalized to be combated. I believe in God, and
I believe in human decency, but above all I
believe that any man's finest hour, is that
moment when he's worked his heart out on a good
cause, and lies exhausted on the field of battle
victorious.

--Vince Lombardi
Football Coach
(1913-1970)

18
Getting Enthusiasm Back In Your Life

People are always blaming their circumstances
for what they are. I don't believe in
circumstances. The people who get on in this
world are the people who get up and look for
the circumstances they want. And if they can't
find them, they make them.

--George Bernard Shaw
English Dramatist
(1856-1950)

Fear Teaching

Why do people lose their positive mental attitudes? When did they lose their enthusiasm? Why did they lose it?

You were born with the confidence and enthusiasm you need for the rest of your life. You were born into this world with positive thoughts and you have the capabilities of greatness, if you wish to use them.

As a newborn, you knew not a negative thought. You started out as unbiased, inquisitive, ready, and unafraid to take chances. You had, as a child, tremendous energy and were undaunted by mistakes. You got right up if you fell down. You tried again, as if failure was supposed to happen along the way.

When most of us look at one-year-olds, we see the purity of life and joy in their bright eyes. We love children's innocence and their openness they bring to life. They have not yet learned the prejudice and hatred, that adults all too often carry in their hearts.

A child will soon be taught negative attitudes about others and himself. Adults all too soon will teach children not to take chances, to avoid being risk-takers. While trying to teach children to be safe, we instill in them negative thoughts about themselves and scare them into feeling inferior and afraid.

A young child begins life fearing nothing or at least only those things that cause pain. Adults soon start teaching children to fear almost everything. A child's day is often filled with a lot of negative messages where adults are saying, "No, don't do that"; "No, don't go there"; and "no, no, no." Some of this teaching is good in order to prevent a child from being harmed or killed. But problems arise later in life because adults have programmed children to think fear first, while never teaching them the type of thinking it takes in order to be successful.

Successful thinking is really the opposite of fear-thinking, but many people never learn how to make the transition to successful thinking. You need to realize that a great amount of emphasis was placed on fear-teaching. You were not born with as much fear as you now have. Fear teaching easily leads into negative thinking about every aspect of life.

Your challenge is to reprogram your thinking, to remove the negative attitudes and negative ways of thinking that you were taught.

Slowly reprogram your subconscious mind to think positive, confident thoughts, which you now know can then be released as positive impulses to your conscious mind.

It was Charles Kettering, an American inventor and automotive manufacturer, who said, "The only time you can't afford to fail is the last time you try."

Make sure you program your mind with those ever-so-important positive statements that will program your subconscious into believing, such as: "This is going to be a great day. I will succeed. I will not shy away from any opportunity here on. As God shows me love, I, too, learn to give unconditional love to all I come in contact with. I will change the world by beginning with me. This is going to be my best presentation ever and these people are going to be glad that they met me."

To be successful, the self-suggestion must be:

1- Believable.

2- Reasonable. It must be within your ability to make it happen. An impossible task will not be accepted by the subconscious.

3- The subconscious mind must be convinced by reaffirming positive thoughts, by "selling" yourself about why your life and the world around you are positive experiences.

Let me present an example of a self-suggestion that can help you: "I feel fantastic!" Then you say, "You know I really do feel fantastic because I'm alive. I'm healthy. I'm free. I can talk. I can see. I've got my mind, and no matter what happens - no one can take this away from me. I really do feel fantastic."

Not doing more than the average
is what keeps the average down.
                    --William M. Winans
                    Philosopher

Abraham Lincoln said, "I do the very best I know how-the very best I can; and I mean to keep on doing so until the end."

John Ratzenberger, the know-it-all mailman named Cliff on the hit TV series *Cheers*, landed the acting job on the show only after failing to land a part at an audition. Up that point in his career, he'd never made it big. He was unknown and just a couple of years earlier was struggling to scrape together enough for a meal. After failing his audition for a part on the *Cheers* series, he said to himself, "I failed already; what do I have to lose at this point?"

He asked the *Cheers* executives at the audition, "Do you have a know-it-all at the bar yet?" The <u>Cheers</u> people said, "What?" He replied, "You know, a know-it-all; every bar has a know-it-all at their bar!" At that point, he proceeded to improvise, using office furniture as props and showing the show's executives the kind of character he was talking about. The *Cheers* executives laughed at the character and a few days later told John that they were interested in his character, but for only a few shows.

The rest is history. The show aired for more than ten years and John Ratzenberger, a struggling, balding actor, wound up on the show for the full duration. He turned out to be a very accomplished actor who found wealth and prestige all because he went the extra mile. He put aside his fear of rejection and presented the executives with something they didn't even know they needed.

John used a form of inspirational dissatisfaction. He did not give up on the first try. His belief in himself and what he had to offer led to the once-in-a-lifetime role.

Do you have the nerve and the confidence not to give up? After failing in one audition, he came up with an impromptu performance and a new idea for the executives.

A failure is never the end. It simply means you have to reprogram yourself to do more creative, positive thinking in order to find the right way to do something successfully. If you give up too soon, you are likely giving in to those childhood voices that keep telling you, "Don't do that" and "No, no, no!"

Vince Lombardi once said, "Winning is not a sometime thing. It is an all time thing. You don't win once in a while, you don't do things right once in a while, you do them right all the time. There is no room for second place..."

Moving to First Place

People like to remember the first place winners or they like to remember the underdog who tried with all his heart to win, but didn't win. We like to root for the underdog in life. We know he will try his hardest to win. There are a lot of people who are the underdog, but they have not learned to get past their fears and try harder to win. Everyone has the same opportunity to win, but winning usually goes to the ones who want it more. It really is that simple.

A popular saying goes, "The eyes are the windows to the soul." Your eyes can project fear, anger, hostility, happiness, laughter, disappointment, friendship, love, sadness, and more. You don't have to be smart to understand the emotions another person is feeling. A child soon learns to sense your emotions from your eyes. You'll notice a child staring at your eyes as soon as you say something. Even a child that you've never met before will look into your eyes for approval, acceptance, or to see if you are angry.

A child can read your emotions without a word being spoken. A dog will even look right into your eyes. There seems to be an innate way that animals and humans try to communicate.

With this in mind, look and pay special attention to the eyes. In most children's eyes, you should see a happy, carefree, and an enthusiastic look. It's worth repeating that a child is born enthusiastic and fearless, feeling capable of leaping tall buildings in a single bound, along with Superman.

Too much fear-teaching leads to a person developing negative thoughts and traits: shyness, poor self-image, indecisiveness, complaining, and a give-up attitude. Adults need to teach children that it's not wrong to be wrong and that failure can be a good thing. We need to teach children to be risk-takers and not to give up, because finding success never comes to you as a piece of paper with a guarantee on it. Children have to be encouraged to learn that the final goal may be achieved only after 10,000 steps are taken in the wrong direction. Remember Thomas Edison's experiments in creating the light bulb?

Reprogram yourself to minimize the fears and the accompanying self-doubts that you still carry from your childhood, after you were taught to fear. Start to destroy your self-doubts.

Immediately begin acting more enthusiastically, even if it is an act. After twenty days, you will have begun a new life, and that new <u>habit</u> will be formed. That new life based on a new way of thinking will lead you to new success.

Let's go back in time, let's think like a baby, where no bad thoughts enter your mind and where there is unconditional love. Minimize your past pain, failures, and negative thoughts. This is the new enthusiastic you!

Today you can't wait to live that new life, much like a child who sees the world with bright eyes, expecting great things to happen. Discover a new child in you who has been hidden behind the negative thoughts and fear that were all forced upon them over the years. Once you start experiencing the world with positive and creative thoughts, the world becomes yours. You cannot be held back.

If a man is called to be a street sweeper,
he should sweep streets even as Michelangelo
painted, or Beethoven composed music,
or Shakespeare wrote poetry. He should sweep
streets so well that all the hosts of heaven
and earth will pause to say, here lived a
great street sweeper who did his job well.

--Martin Luther King Jr.
Civil Rights Leader
(1929-1968)

19
Faith In Yourself

No man... ever made himself a leader in sports,
or in life, without doing a great deal of hard
work... It is not an easy road, but it is an
eminently satisfactory road, because it leads to
the desired end.

--Walter S. Camp
Football Coach
(1859-1925)

Can't Do It?

I've often heard the phrase used for athletes and musicians, "They were born with natural talent." I know that some people can sing better than others and some can play baseball better than many others. Granted, some people are born with physical advantage that may be better suited for certain sports, such as above average height, weight, or bone structure which will make it a little easier for a person to succeed in a given sport.

More importantly though is the athlete who loves his given sport and has a desire to succeed. When a person has a true burning desire, he can compete against the best. A burning desire drives an individual, pushing him to greatness.

It's a well-known fact that many Olympic athletes practice ten to twelve hours every day for many years in preparation for the Olympic games. Now think about this: If you were to practice a given sport with the proper attitude for ten hours a day and were strengthening your body over the years, don't you think that you, too, could excel in the sport? Maybe you would not be the best, but perhaps you would be in the top ten percent of all the players in the game.

This brings to mind a professional baseball player named Jim Abbott who played for the New York Yankees. Jim was born with only one hand – his left. Picture yourself trying to play professional baseball with the great players in the major leagues and being able to use only your left hand.

Jim Abbott was a starting pitcher for the Yanks. He usually pitched about eight innings a game. Not only could he play the game, which is remarkable in itself, but Abbott was also a very good pitcher.

How did he do it? Well, what he did was catch the ball from the catcher with his glove on his left hand. He then held the glove against his right limb, the stub with no hand. Then, with the limb resting against the glove, he'd wind up and pitch the ball. As soon as he had thrown the ball, he would slip his left hand into the glove. Abbott, believe it or not, could actually pitch the ball with one hand and field the ball very well if it was hit back to him.

Talk about "burning desire" and faith in oneself! He was in the Major Leagues for many years starting in 1989, and in September 4, 1993 he even pitched a no hitter against the Cleveland Indians. It's amazing what some people can do when they want something badly enough.

If you think you can't do something, think about Jim Abbott. "All things are possible as long as you long for it enough!" By changing your attitudes, you will change your results.

If you wish to become very successful in anything, you must first realize that you cannot be extremely successful in every aspect of your life. No athlete can excel in all sports.

My mentor and friend, Bob Richards, the great Olympic gold medal champion who graced the cover of the Wheaties Cereal box, said, "Ingenuity, plus courage, plus work, equals miracles."

Things That You Have

The other day I realized how truly blessed most of us are. While working on a household project, I had cut my right thumb with a utility blade. The razor-sharp blade cut my thumb so deeply that I had to have it stitched in the emergency room of the local hospital. After it was wrapped, I could not use the most important finger on the hand that I use all the time, my right hand.

I did not appreciate the importance of my right thumb, until I could not use it. I soon realized the importance of my right thumb for shaving, brushing my teeth, writing, buttoning my shirt, and in dressing. Life became a little more frustrating without my right thumb to help me.

This experience made me realize how fortunate most of us are because we are blessed with all our senses and body parts. I cannot speak for a handicapped person, but I believe success is a little easier to achieve if we have all our senses and body parts working normally.

The other day I saw a story on television about a man who was born with no arms. I felt rather foolish at that moment complaining about the temporary loss of my right thumb. As I continued to watch this young man with no arms, I saw a totally self-sufficient man. Granted he didn't have arms, but still this young man managed to brush his teeth. He drove a car, opened a jar, drank, ate, and did everything I could do, all by using his two feet in place of his arms and hands. By raising his leg up the way we use our arms, this man did it all. I found it amazing how he could function rather quickly without arms. He drove his own car to different locations and gave speeches to young students on the subject of achieving success and maintaining a positive attitude. He also demonstrated to the young people that, if he could be successful with his limitations, then they could apply their healthy minds and bodies to achieve success as well.

George Allen, former coach of the Washington Redskins, summed it up best when he said, "God gave every single human being a certain amount of talent, and unless you utilize that talent to the utmost of your ability twenty-four hours of every day of your life, you deceive your God, your family, and above all yourself."

I had the immense pleasure in hearing Gerald Coffee speak in person at a sales convention several years ago. Gerald Coffee is a retired Navy captain who, while flying a mission over North Vietnam on February 3, 1966, had his plane shot down.

Trying to get as far out to sea as possible, with hopes of being rescued, Captain Coffee put the throttles forward, but the aircraft did not respond, instead it rolled out of control. He and his crew ejected, but landed in the water only about half a mile from the coast of North Vietnam. They were immediately captured by the Vietnamese. After being placed in a Vietnamese boat, they were almost killed when the boat was shot at by a couple of American fighters from the aircraft carrier Kitty Hawk, whose pilots thought they were firing only on Vietnamese soldiers.

After several passes, the firing stopped. Captain Coffee ended up twelve days later at a POW camp in Hanoi at which time he learned that his crewmen had been killed during the capture.

Captain Coffee had a few broken bones he sustained as he'd ejected from the plane. Now, he had to face living in a prison cell that was only seven feet long by three feet wide. He, along with the others in the prison, had to suffer through brutal experiences. He suffered through a long series of tortures and interrogations.

His only communication with fellow prisoners was a tapping signal system because talking was not allowed. The tapping had to be done very carefully because the "no communication" rule was harshly enforced. Beatings were a regular occurrence as the guards routinely tried to extract any information they could from their prisoners.

Through seven years and nine days of no verbal communications, Captain Coffee survived the whole ordeal by maintaining his faith in God and a faith that he would survive. Here are Gerald Coffee's own words, "I'd come to realize that the key to my survival all those years was simply, faith. Now, I know that when I say faith, we automatically tend to think of spiritual, religious faith. And that's natural, because that's the vehicle by which most of us believe in things we can't touch or hear or see. You have to take them on faith, as they say. But in this context, I realized that there were four aspects of faith.

"First of all, there was faith in ourselves as individuals. Faith in myself there in the prisons in North Vietnam to simply recognize and pursue my duty, seldom perfectly, but always to the very best of my ability. The second aspect of faith was faith in one another, faith in the people around me. Faith in the people with whom we work each day, faith in the people we love. The third aspect of faith was faith in my country, America, faith in her basic institutions, our national purpose and cause at any given time. And the fourth aspect of faith, of course, was faith in my

God, maybe the foundation for it all."

Faith became Captain Coffee's means for surviving a torturous 2,550 day period of no verbal communication with anyone, except for the tapping communication system, which often had to be done between the swishing sounds of a broom, coughing, and other improvised sounds. It took minutes just to tap out a single word. But, nonetheless, the prisoners still managed to communicate with each other, giving one another hope and faith.

After hearing Captain Coffee's inspiring talk, I felt that I could accomplish anything. He showed that we're all made the same and, when necessary, we can all look deep within ourselves and find the strength to withstand worse things that may come our way.

Captain Coffee showed himself to be an American hero. We all need heroes. Heroes inspire us. They convince us that we too can do something special. Heroes stand out from the average person in the crowd.

I believe that one of the great freedoms in America is the freedom to control your destiny. That means you can change your life immediately.

Captain Coffee will tell you that most people take for granted all the freedoms and good things in America. If you observe what life is like in other countries with less freedom, you should not have to be reminded about how great life can be in America.

Your faith is waiting to be used. Don't wait for something drastic to happen before putting your faith to work. You hold within yourself, at this very moment, all the faith you need to get you through the toughest situation you may face.

Believe in yourself. Believe in your fellow man, because the majority of people want a peaceful, happy life as much as you do. Believe in America and its ideals. People still want to come to America, some even risking their lives to come here on homemade boats to reach America's shores.

Renew your faith in yourself and your abilities. You will automatically achieve extraordinary results with more faith in yourself.

The important thing is not to stop questioning. Curiosity has it's own reason for existing. One cannot help but be in awe when he contemplates the mysteries of eternity, of life, of the marvelous structure of reality. It is enough if one tries merely to comprehend a little of this mystery every day. Never lose a holy curiosity.

--Albert Einstein
Physicist
(1878-1955)

21
Burning Desire

If one advances confidently in the direction of his dreams, and endeavors to live the life which he has imagined, he will meet with a success unexpected in common hours.

--Henry Thoreau
Essayist/Poet
(1817-1862)

Bigger Ideas Are Possible

Did you know that the person who invented the paper clip earned a whopping $500,000. Not bad for a small piece of metal bent into a unique shape. But, more importantly, another person who changed and improved the paper clip made $750,000. He made three quarters of a million dollars for improving on an existing, proven idea. That proves you don't always have to be first person to come up with a brilliant new idea. You can in fact be very successful at improving upon an existing product or idea.

If you look at a company like Sony, it is consistently coming up with great ideas such as the Walkman cassette player, the Beta Max, and the CD Walkman. After a new product is invented, others immediately modify and improve on the ideas, then produce and market their new versions of the original product.

Many simple inventions are nothing more than common sense ideas which solve minor inconveniences or improve upon products already on the market.

Ray Kroc, the marketing genius behind the McDonald's franchise operation, was born in 1902. In 1922, at age 20, he was employed as a salesman selling Lily brand paper cups to businesses. In 1937, at age 35, Ray Kroc sold all his possessions and bought the distribution for Multi Mixing Machines. They were mixers that made great milk shakes, which Ray sold to restaurant owners.

One day, Kroc came across the McDonald brothers hamburgers stand. He immediately fell in love with the fast-food business that the McDonald brothers had going, and which was unique to the restaurant industry at that time. Ray proposed to the McDonalds an idea where he would take their business of fast food hamburgers and fries and market it as a franchise across America.

In 1955 at age 52, Ray Kroc opened his first McDonald's franchise. By 1960, there were 200 franchise operations going. Ray then paid the McDonalds 2.7 million dollars for their entire operation.

Today, the McDonald's corporation has its own school, The Hamburger University, where new franchise owners come to learn the fast food business and the McDonald's money-making system.

In the 1990's, there were 14,000 McDonald's stores in some 70 countries and there were over one million employees working worldwide in the operations. Today, there's even a McDonald's in Russia.

Who would have imagined that a paper cup salesman could accomplish so much? If Ray Kroc had not had the vision, the McDonald brothers' hamburger stand might have remained one small store. But, Kroc had the vision of something bigger in his mind that others never saw or thought possible. He also believed the concept he had in his mind would catch on.

Your Burning Desire Can Affect Others

There are some people who are addicts in the streets or burned out mentally and some who are left with no hope or motivation to help themselves. Although it is encouraging to know that some of those people can be rescued and ultimately returned to a productive life, there are those who have just given up on life and on themselves. Those who live self-destructive lives are not offering any positives to the world. They are influencing others mostly in negative ways.

You can make a difference. You can have a positive effect.

The more good that you do, the more you are helping the world. I believe that doing good has a geometric affect because the good that you do ultimately affects thousands of others with whom you have no direct contact.

The whole world is influenced by you, both directly and indirectly. You have the power and the ability to touch many people in very special ways. The good that you do is impossible to track, but you can be assured it can reach everyone from the children to the elderly.

Remember: your actions, attitudes, and words are absorbed by the subconscious minds of everyone who hears and sees you, and will affect them, positively or negatively. By keeping that in mind, you can motivate yourself to modify your behavior and attitude towards others you come in contact with. Think of it as being on stage each time you say something. You can affect someone else's attitude, whether in a good or bad way. You can change another person's life.

Our lives, no matter how plain and boring they may seem, are important to many people, loved ones, co-workers, and strangers. Don't ever take your life for granted. Don't ever feel that you have little value and that you are unimportant. You are the greatest living miracle on earth.

Start acting as if your next actions will change someone's life for the better. Make believe that PBS is shooting a week-long documentary about how your positive attitudes and your life have helped to change the lives of others. Make believe the camera is rolling. How will you act?

You can, in fact, act dramatically differently – be positive. Try it. See how quickly people respond to the extra-positive you. It is contagious. You'll see.

I found out that there are now more than 30,000 people in the U.S. who are over the age of 100. That's an amazing statistic. It was rare for anyone to make it to age 100 just a few decades ago and now there are over 30,000. Granted, some of these 30,000 may be in failing health, but I guarantee you that a good many of them have sharp enough minds such that they can remember back 90 years to their youth.

I've seen interviews with some 100-plus year olds and have been surprised at the sharpness of their memories. Imagine the number of people these people may have influenced over the years. Your positive attitudes and success may have an impact on hundreds or thousands of others you may never meet. Your greatness will impact on thousands of others.

Jean Rostand, the 19th century biologist, said, "A man is not old as long as he is seeking something."

Michelangelo, the great Italian Renaissance artist, said, "Lord, grant that I may always desire more than I can accomplish." He lived to age 89 and he certainly is an example of someone who has influenced and inspired millions of people centuries after his death.

If you accomplish many positive things in life and go on to succeed beyond where you are now, you could very likely influence many people long after you are gone. Your burning desire can light up someone else's heart that will help him or her to be successful too.

I remember one of my special victories when I had a tremendous burning desire to pass a certain license exam, which required two months of study. The license was very important to me.

I knew the exam would be very difficult because most people failed this type of test the first time they took it. I decided to skip the required and rigorous school course, and I received permission to self-study for the exam without the course. But, I had to take the exam before a certain cutoff date.

For weeks, I practiced repeated positive self-affirmations. I kept telling myself, "I must pass this exam. I cannot fail this test, and I must study every chance I get. I must pass now!"

Through positive self-suggestions, with strong emotions, I etched into my subconscious mind the urgency of the goal. After accepting the urgency, my subconscious started to release impulses to my conscious mind. In this case, the urgency of remembering the information was real and important to me, and I would stop at nothing until I had passed the exam.

I did pass that test on my first attempt. I found that amazing since I did it through self-study. I had been consumed with that goal. There was no such thing as failure in my mind.

That exam represented for me the big difference between a simple want and a true burning desire. The burning desire is all-consuming, and one your subconscious mind just can't let go, even while you sleep. All great accomplishments stem from that *intense* burning desire.

You can achieve greatness. You must be willing to pay the price to attain such success. What do you want? What is the burning desire deep inside you? When you get very serious about achieving a goal, write it down, and plan how to attain it. The burning desire starts to become more real, and an all-important drive to accomplish that goal takes over.

Be careful not to turn all your wants and small goals into burning desires. Keep your burning desires open to only those special dreams and goals. Focus on the major burning desires and success will be yours each and every time.

Joel Barker, an American author, said, "Vision without action is merely a dream. Action without vision just passes the time. Vision with action can change the world."

I am intrigued by buildings and the construction of homes. I marvel at an idea on paper, the blueprint that turns out to be a strong, well-constructed home that stands for a hundred years or more. Many times I will follow the construction progress of a local building, watching the process that starts with clearing a piece of property.

Success is like the building of a home. You can't start with the roof, which I would call the monetary gain of success. You must begin with a strong plan, the blueprint. Goals are similar to the foundation of the home. The foundation is certainly the most important part of the structure. If the concrete is inferior or poorly mixed, the foundation can crack. If your plans for success are not well thought out, you have no blueprint for success.

Successful people do the tasks that unsuccessful people fail to do. That foundation, without a doubt, must be perfectly level and square. The entire structure is dependent on resting on that foundation. The home must withstand snow, ice, storms, and winds of at least a hundred miles per hour.

Life is like a home. Its blueprint and foundation must be sound. This book also had a blueprint. It took many hours of planning just for the first word to be printed. I would estimate that over one thousand hours were invested in this project before it was published. An overwhelming effort? Yes, but the time and effort were needed to accomplish the goal of a published book. Despite the massive amount of work, the emphasis is on the benefits derived and used by the readers.

This is an illustration of the driving force, the all-consuming urge that keeps the successful person pushing on. I would never deny that there will always be obstacles, even some rather large ones, but each obstacle is carefully and systematically pushed aside. You can build a house based on your own blueprint of goals. You've already accomplished smaller goals and projects.

Be consumed. Be driven. Keep your eye on the finish line. But never, never ever give up. Build that dream goal today.

In the middle of every difficulty
lies opportunity.

> *--Albert Einstein*
> *Physicist*
> *(1879-1955)*

21
Remembering Where You Came From

*Every tradition grows ever more venerable -
the more remote is its origin, the more
confused that origin is. The reverence due
to it increases from generation to
generation. The tradition finally becomes
holy and inspires awe.*

--Friedrich Wilhelm Nietzsche
German Philosopher
(1844-1900)

Looking Back to Look Forward

When is the last time you thought about your grandfather's grandfather? I want you to remember where you came from, but not just in terms of location and relatives. I want you to go back in time in your mind. Try to picture life as it was some one hundred fifty or two hundred years ago.

If your grandfather was born in 1895 and his grandfather was born in 1835, that is not a long time in history. Most people remember one or both of their grandparents, but few of us have known any family relatives older than our grandparents.

America has always been the land of immigrants, where so many Americans have family ties to other countries. Some families have relatives in other countries that they've never met.

In my family, I know that my grandfather came to America from Italy while a young man. He raised a family in America, but never went back to visit Italy. For most of my life, I had never thought about my grandfather's grandfather. But for the purpose of this experiment, I would like to try to understand life as it was back in 1835.

In the eighteen hundreds, the moods and attitudes at that time were much different. My grandfather's grandfather did not have television or radio to inform, entertain him, or to waste his day away. All of his information came from reading and conversation. There were no modern conveniences. If someone wanted a hot bath, he had to manually heat the water. If he wanted to go somewhere, he had to hitch a horse and buggy and take a rather bumpy ride, that is, if he was fortunate enough to own a horse. Most people could not travel very far.

Although life in the eighteen hundreds was totally different from today, I believe it was satisfying and pleasant in its simplicity. Even though we have vastly improved our lifestyle, I have to wonder whether we are more content.

Today, our modern jets compress travel time down to hours. We can travel to almost any place on earth or use cell phones to call anyone anywhere around the globe. With the information in our biggest libraries and access to the Internet, we have the capability to acquire much more information than people from 1835. But, has this information made us smarter in the ways we are living? We have had two major wars in the last century that have killed millions of people. How "smart" are we if our weapons of mass destruction can kill millions of people and we're willing to use those weapons on each other?

I also wonder whether too many people have lost an appreciation of the work ethic and wait for a hand-delivered ticket to an easy life.

An excerpt from The Recreations Of A Country Parson by A. Spoi gives an idea about life in 1867:

"Just at my gate, the man who keeps in order the roads of the parish was hard at work. How pleasant, I thought, to work amid the pure air and sweet smelling clover.

"I inquired how his wife and children were. I asked how he liked the new cottage he had lately moved into. 'Well,' he said. But it was far from his work: he had walked eight miles and a half that morning to his work; he had to walk the same distance home again in the evening after labouring all day; and for this his wages were thirteen shillings a week, with a deduction for such days as he might be unable to work. He did not mention all this by way of complaint; he was comfortably off, he said; he should be thankful he was so much better off than many."

Imagine trying to walk eight miles to work today and walk eight miles back home. Do you really understand how easy you have it today compared to life around 1835?

Back in those days of the 1800s, people worked very hard from early dawn until sunset. We have to respect what they accomplished without the luxury of electricity, computers, and electronic gadgets. Today, electricity gives us the freedom to work late into the evening or to spend time doing nothing more than watching television shows.

It's easy to take our modern conveniences for granted, that is until the electricity goes off. Without electricity, we're literally left in the dark. Our light bulbs go out; none of our appliances and computers work. Our "modern" world almost totally shuts down without electricity. For the most part, it's electricity that keeps us living in the modern age with all our conveniences. Without electricity, we are living just as our grandfathers' grandfathers had to live. The next time you are without electricity you might have an idea what life was like, not only in 1835, but daily living in all the past centuries without electricity.

How you use electricity may even depend on how successful you will be. You may be wasting time watching too much television or you may be wisely using electricity to study at nights in order to do more with your life.

After reading <u>The Recreations Of A Country Parson</u>, I now have a fairly good understanding about the simplicity of life in the eighteenth century. The author, the parson of a small country church, tells how he passes the time and expresses his feelings about many things of his time. Here is another excerpt from the book showing how you don't necessarily have to have today's technology to be happy:

"This is a Monday morning. It is a beautiful sun shiny morning early in July. I am sitting on the steps that lead to my door, somewhat tired by the duty of yesterday, but feeling very restful and thankful. Before me there is a little expanse of the brightest grass, very soft and mossy, and very carefully mown. It is shaded by three noble beeches, about two hundred years old. The sunshine around has a green tinge from the reflection of the leaves. Double hedges, thick and tall, the inner one of gleaming beech shut out all sight of a country lane that runs hard by: a lane into which this graveled sweep of would be - avenue enters, after winding deftly through evergreens, rich and old, so as to make the utmost of its little length... .

"You kneel down and pray by the bedside of many sick; and you know the look of the dying face well. Young children, whom you have humbly sought to instruct in the best of knowledge, have passed away from this life in your presence, telling you in interrupted sentences whither they trusted they were going, and bidding you not to forget to meet them there... .

"And when you ride up the parish on your way to duty, you feel the influence of the bare and lonely tracts, where, ten miles from home, you sometimes dismount from your horse, and sit down on a gray stone by the wayside, and look for an hour at the heather at your feet, and the sweeps of purple moorland far away..."

That book was a tremendous find for me while on vacation in Ireland. I enjoyed the simplicity and unique history of the 1800s. Reading about that parson's life helped me to appreciate life more than ever. Perhaps, the older we get the more deeply we view life and all its wonders. From my readings of such books as the parson's, I realize that each new day is a special gift, and once it's gone, we can't live that day again.

Life With No Regrets

Each morning, I awake to the light that shines through a large six foot Palladian window in my bedroom. While in my bed and slowly waking to the new day, I repeat the same following statement, "Thank you, Lord, for this glorious and new day. I don't know why I have been given this gift of a new day when others, far smarter and more gifted than me have been taken away from this world. Others, who have contributed much more to mankind than me have not been offered this precious day.

"I vow to make the most of this new and exciting day. I will not waste this special gift you have given. I vow also to be kinder and gentler to all I see today. I will do more today than yesterday. I know that tomorrow is not guaranteed to the richest king, so I must work with what I have. I will not let you down, Lord, in giving me this new day of life. This will be the best day of my life. And, if I'm fortunate to have another day, I vow that it will be even better."

These are more positive self-suggestions for your subconscious. Keep your brain working on the positive. Never stop the positive statements.

The fear of wasting my God-given talents drives me forward and keeps me wanting to be productive and successful.

Life is an opportunity, benefit from it.

Life is beauty, admire it.

Life is bliss, taste it.

Life is a dream, realize it.

Life is a challenge, meet it.

Life is a duty, complete it.

Life is a game, play it.

Life is a promise, fulfill it.

Life is sorrow, overcome it.

Life is a song, sing it.

Life is a struggle, accept it.

Life is a tragedy, confront it.

Life is an adventure, dare it.

Life is luck, make it.

Life is too precious, do not destroy it.

Life is life, fight for it.

--Mother Teresa

22
Don't Be Nonchalant About Life

*The worst bankrupt in the world is the
person who has lost his enthusiasm.*

--H.W. Arnold

Philosopher

Throughout this book I've shared with you many things that have helped me through my life and my career thus far. One of the most important things I've learned is, "You can't be nonchalant about life and succeed."

Everybody loves a winner. And many of the winners I've met and read about were hard working, very positive individuals where the words "fail" and "can't" do not enter their minds. Similar to the technique I've used to program my mind to eliminate all foul and abusive language, very successful people of the past and present have programmed their minds not to accept negativity, pessimism, or failure. To be a winner, you must think like a winner.

All actors must practice continuously before going in front of an audience or before the camera. Athletes in all sports must practice, practice, practice. Basketball players, minutes before the game starts, can be seen on the court, practicing and taking shots.

In the Olympic games, I've seen figure skaters warming up minutes before skating in a competition. For the Olympics, the athletes take four years to prepare for what may only be a few minutes of competition. One slip, one fall, and the chance of an Olympic medal is lost. You can't be nonchalant about being prepared. You can't fool around and expect to be successful. Champion athletes get to the top after years of hard work, dedication, and concentration. In fact, all serious endeavors, both big and small, require hard work, focus and attention.

Before I started in sales, I was working at a lumber company advising customers about their home improvements. That was the first time I realized that I could motivate people to do things I suggested.

I did well at the lumber company. Every day after school and all day on Saturdays, I stocked shelves, swept floors, and did everything I was told to do. Before long, I moved up to counter sales and began ordering all the store's hardware. What I liked about the job was, for the first time in my life, I felt powerful.

By helping people design wood projects, kitchen cabinet jobs, and also helping them choose paneling for their walls, I felt in control. I felt that I could convince the buyer to buy a certain color or particular brand, or build their project a certain way. I worked at convincing the customer to act based on my recommendations, for what was in his or her best interest.

So, at age twenty, I felt fairly confident in taking a life insurance sales position. Life insurance sales is harder than most sales positions because the salesperson is selling a piece of paper, a promise, and the solution to a problem that the prospective customer never realized he or she had.

Many sales people fail in the insurance business. At first, I didn't do well. I learned some hard lessons and made up my mind that I could not afford to fail in the business. The key to my success, and it seemed frightening at first, was that I knew I had to succeed at selling insurance. I was not trained for many other occupations. I had a tremendous desire to succeed. I simply didn't want the alternative -- a mediocre job in another field.

For more than a quarter century, I have found there is a great deal of satisfaction in protecting someone's family, while making a good living. I don't sell as much now, but rather have brokers selling for my agency.

I always felt that I had to work harder than the next person just to get the same results, but work never scared me.

Today, I'm motivated to learn all I can about my business and about new opportunities in life. It's amazing to me that, as a teenager, I thought life would be so simple. If I could go back and change a couple of things in life, I would certainly be a lot more serious about getting a better education.

The point is that you cannot be nonchalant about life. You will do better if you have a rudder with which to steer yourself and a compass to guide you on your way. The average person will let the wind blow him around, which could be in circles. Those who learn to take positive control of their thinking and go beyond the standards of the average person are the ones who have a direction and a destination that will take them to the shores of success.

In life, you need to enjoy your job since you spend so much time there each week, and you will likely have to work about 45 or more years before you can retire. Not only should the job be satisfying, it should also be challenging and not too simple or boring.

I believe most of us had parents who did all they could to help us. As a child, I can remember there was never a time when I caught my mother sleeping. I don't think that mothers with small children actually do sleep. Every time I got up not feeling well in the middle of the night, my mother heard me and was there for me.

Most parents would sacrifice their own lives to keep their children alive. As I mentioned before, my father worked three jobs to support his wife and five children. My hardworking parents remind me that most of us owe a lot to our parents who have sacrificed in many ways to help us.

You owe it to your parents and yourself to be as successful as you can.

People who are nonchalant about life are insulting their parents, who may have scrimped and saved, worked extra jobs to put them through school.

You are a great miracle. Excel now! Act like the miracle you are. Now is your time to become great. I know I have tremendous desire to achieve greatness -- for all those who count on me.

Your greatness will influence and inspire others in great ways too.

The harder the conflict, the more glorious the triumph. What we obtain too cheap, we esteem too lightly; it is dearness only that gives everything its value. I love the man that can smile in trouble, that can gather strength from distress and grow brave by reflection. 'Tis the business of little minds to shrink; but he whose heart is firm, and whose conscience approves his conduct, will pursue his principles unto death.

--Thomas Paine
Political Leader
(1737-1809)

Total Relaxation Technique

Just as your mind needs to feed positive statements to your subconscious, it is, also, extremely important to relax your mind. Give it a "vacation" of sorts.

The best way I've found to totally relax the mind is to erase everything it senses for a few minutes. I call this "mind cleansing," a way to calm down the mind. Thus, a calm mind calms down the body, heart rate, and blood pressure. But more importantly, you are cleansing your mind of the stresses, worries, and pressures that have built up in it.

The best time to do this exercise is twenty minutes before you fall asleep.

Start by lying down on a bed with total silence around you. It could be light, but a darker room helps the eyes to relax better.

You want to start with your eyes. Think of them as fully relaxed and getting heavy. Feel each muscle of the eyes slowly unwind and relax. Then, think of your arms. Again, they are heavier and each muscle is relaxing. After a minute, move on to your legs, feet, and stomach. Only move on if you feel totally relaxed in each part of the body. You can feel your mind clearing already.

Once you have relaxed your entire body, you will work on your mind. Next, picture in full detail your car or your family's car. Think of the shape size and color of the car. For a full thirty seconds, visualize that car all over.

Next, visualize your spouse's or friend's eyes. See the color. Study them, looking at all the colors you believe that you are seeing. Look at the iris.

Next, make believe you are staring up at the bluest sky and the puffiest white cloud formations you ever saw. Don't move from the sky until you see the color blue. Then, move on to the white, three-dimensional clouds. See all the shades of white, as if you are attempting to paint them.

Next, I want you to look out over the clearest beach, studying the sand. Slowly move your vision to the waves cascading in and move to look out over the ocean as far as you can see. Look at a couple of seagulls in the sky. Spend a full two minutes looking at this ocean and beach scene. Study the water.

It's important not to give into falling off to sleep just yet. There's a state just before sleep that I want you to remain in as long as you can. You'll know this state as soon as you feel it. It feels like bliss, like what heaven must feel like. It's as if you were legally high. Maintain that feeling as long as you can. That feeling of euphoria is so unique that it will shock you at first. You'll remember it, but you will probably fall asleep too fast. Work on it for a few nights, work until you can master that euphoric state and try to stay in it for a while.

It is not unusual, once in this state, to feel like you have risen out of your body for a short while. The whole point is to give your body and mind a total relaxation therapy session.

You will have mastered the technique when you are in a state of euphoria and feel like not a muscle in your body is awake or able to respond. You will fall into the deepest sleep you have had in quite some time.

If man has good corn, or wood, or boards,
or pigs to sell, or can make better chairs
or knives, crucibles, or church organs,
than anybody else, you will find a broad,
hard-beaten road to his house, tho it be
in the woods.

> *--Ralph Waldo Emerson*
> *Essayist/Poet*
> *(1803-1882)*

23
The Power Of Belief

*The man who decides what he wants to achieve and
works till his dreams all come true,
the man who will alter his course when he must and
bravely begin something new,
the man who's determined to make his world better,
who's willing to learn and to lead,
the man who keeps trying and doing his best is the
man who knows how to succeed.*

--Author Unknown

Belief in yourself, a cause, or in your ability to overcome an obstacle is a very powerful force. A strong belief in what you want to accomplish is very important for being able to complete your goals.

You exercise a belief in your abilities every day. While driving, you believe in your abilities to park in a tight space or to handle the car in an emergency situation in order to avoid an accident.

Your belief in yourself started in childhood when you learned to ride a bicycle, make something, or compete with others.

As an adult, you have had to extend your beliefs in yourself. You learned specific tasks that help you do your work. As you grew more confident, you believed you could do more.

Without belief, a conviction that you can do what you set your mind to do, you will have a hard time succeeding in anything.

The slightest bit of doubt in yourself can become an unnecessary obstacle. Your own negativity can destroy your momentum in accomplishing your greatness, even though you are a capable person.

You can expand your "belief-in-yourself" attitude to all facets of your life by conditioning your mind into believing that you will not fail and that you will succeed in your chosen goals.

Your mind has amazing powers. It's more amazing than any computer because it can create new ideas and its positive powers can help motivate you to accomplish great things in life. When you believe in something, your mind will stop at nothing to bring the successful outcome to pass.

James Russell Lowell said, "Not failure, but low aim, is a crime." It was Oliver Wendell Holmes who said, "A mind once stretched by a new idea never regains its original dimensions."

A woman from Scotland named Ms. Campbell, at age 26, left from Africa in April of 1991 in her quest to walk around the world. By September of 1993, Ms. Campbell had walked more than 17,000 miles through thirteen countries on four continents.

Every goal requires a positive outlook and belief in one's ability to succeed.

Anyone can walk five miles in a day. Many people in Manhattan walk five miles without realizing they're walking that far because so many other sights and people occupy their attention.

Who would want to walk 17,000 miles? That takes a real commitment. When the muscles in the body ache, the person on such a journey has made a deep commitment to keep right on going.

You do not have to walk around the world as Ms. Campbell did, but you are capable of achieving some fantastic goals in your life. Accomplishing every goal requires one step at a time, one day at a time. It takes a great deal of willpower, fortitude, and desire to keep moving forward to reach your goals day after day.

Just like the person who wants to chop down a large tree, the tree will come down, but only after repeated swinging away at the tree. You do not have to make mighty swings to bring down a tree, because small swings of an axe can ultimately bring down the tree too. One drop of water will do nothing to a heavy iron bar, but let the drops continue, one drop at a time, twenty-four hours a day, day after day and, in time, the drops will wear a hole through the iron bar.

Life is no different. Think of success as focusing your energies on one thing at a time with no disruptions.

I remember as a young boy experimenting with a magnifying glass and a piece of paper. I had read how a spot of light shining through the magnifying glass from the sun could burn a hole through the paper. By intensifying the sun's rays, you can produce much greater heat and light.

The laser beam accomplishes a similar result. Lasers have been expanded to be used in all parts of modern life, from the lasers that read bar codes at the check out stands in stores to medical uses.

There are times you need to focus on your goals with your mind having the intensity of a laser. Laser thinking can be useful to accomplishing goals, especially when you have a limited amount of time to finish your goals.

There's a great saying: "If you want to play, you've got to pay." It sounds simple, but makes good sense. If you want a certain promotion at your job, are you willing to pay the price to get that promotion? Do you know what the price is? The price of that promotion may be your having to work late one day, two days, or perhaps everyday. The price may be changing your disposition, attitude, or work habits.

There is always a specific price to pay for every success that you want in life.

Plan out a strategy for attaining your success, but make sure not to overdo your work time to the detriment of hurting your family or your own health. Find the right balance, similar to the carburetor on the car that needs the right mixture of air and gasoline. When working right, the small carburetor can move an eighteen-wheel truck. Without the right mixture, any vehicle will stall and not move one inch.

My philosophy has always been based on a truism, "A happy worker is a productive worker." The home life must come first so that you will _want_ to work and have good reasons as to _why_ you are working hard. You are willing to work hard in order to provide a good life for your family.

In his monthly cassette program <u>Insight,</u> Earl Nightingale, told of the following exercise:

"If this were your last day to live, and you were asked to write a blueprint for living for children, what would you write? What would you tell them that would give them a wise and true course to follow for the rest of their lives?"

<u>Here's what I would tell children:</u>

1- Love all types of people you meet.

2- Always do more for others than they do for you, for it's better to give than to receive.

3- Always build up someone's self-esteem; never tear it down.

4- Always be positive with yourself and others.

Remember, people can always find others who are negative, but a positive, upbeat person is a rare treasure and everyone will be glad that they met you.

5- Remember that the Lord is your shepherd and you do not have to fear.

6- All things are possible through belief in the Lord and yourself, and with His help you can accomplish anything.

7- Never, ever be satisfied; always strive for more. You can be anything you truly want to be.

8- Do not ignore your loved ones.

9- Make each day count. Don't waste your time.

10-The span of a human life is short. Stand out from the crowd by being different and seeking to achieve great results in your life!"

The invention of the crayon is over 100 years old. The Crayola Crayon company has sold over 100 billion crayons since 1903. Someone had tremendous insight to invent a crayon that could be enjoyed by billions of people around the world.

Do you have an idea that could be as popular as the crayon? Be different by thinking different. A successful person who comes up with successful ideas may have ideas as simple as a crayon.

Galileo, who challenged the thinking of his day, said, "You cannot teach a man anything; you can only help him to find it within himself."

On the plains of hesitation bleach the bones
of countless millions who, at the dawn of
victory, sat down to wait, and waiting - died!

--George W. Cecil
American Writer
(1891-1970)

24
Dissatisfaction Accomplishes More

*I have offended God and mankind
because my work didn't reach the
quality it should have.*

> *--Leonardo da Vinci*
> *Florentine Artist and Engineer*
> *(1452-1519)*

Mediocrity Prevents Success

Leonardo da Vinci, one of the world's greatest artists, felt capable of even greater work than he had accomplished. Dissatisfaction can be turned into something good because that feeling motivates you to do better after you've accomplished each goal and you want to make tomorrow's work better than what you did today. Satisfaction can create laziness and can prevent you from striving for greatness.

I'm sure you have stopped too soon in certain endeavors and, by stopping, you've accepted mediocre results. Though acceptable to others, they were not done according to your best ability.

From now on, go the extra mile. Don't ever accept mediocrity again!

Charles Kettering said, "An inventor fails 999 times, and if he succeeds once, he's in. He treats his failures simply as practice shots."

Some people never seem to be satisfied. This dissatisfaction can lead to a higher plateau of successful results. Some individuals want to achieve as many great results during their life that go beyond all the average people. Leonardo da Vinci was that rare person whose work, inventions, and ideas seemed to fit into five lifetimes and who stood as an example of a great achiever, but he kept accomplishing more because he became dissatisfied with each of his great accomplishments.

Once one goal is reached, most of us get dissatisfied and want to reach a greater goal. Every golfer as well as every bowler wants to play a perfect game.

You can only do what your mind believes is possible. If you are seeking a new sports goal, you may have to push your mind to push your body to attain that new goal; however, your mind has to believe that the goal is attainable without any doubts.

As Roger Bannister showed, he knew the four-minute mile could be broken and he wouldn't stop trying until he broke that record.

Only those who dare to fail greatly
can ever achieve greatly.

--Robert F. Kennedy
U.S. Senator and Attorney General
(1925-1968)

New Thinking

Reconditioning your thinking is the act of stretching your mind to realize you are capable of more.

In all sports, there are physical limitations beyond which an athlete's body cannot go. For example, a human could never run a mile in thirty seconds.

When it comes to your mental prowess, you have no limitations when it comes to your mental stretching. You have the mental power to become a billionaire, to make the impossible happen, and to achieve greatness. The more you stretch your thinking the more you accomplish, even if it's something as simple as inventing a crayon that can be used by billions of people.

A salesperson who does not like to do telemarketing to find new prospects may have to make the calls in two sessions. That salesperson may have to start convincing himself through positive self-suggestions that he can make twenty new phone contacts a day. The salesperson may need to give himself positive mental reinforcement by saying, "The best part of my job is the phone contacts, and I get paid extremely well for finding new people."

Through repetitive positive statements like those, the salesperson can actually develop the right outlook that creates better sales. After completing half of the necessary calls, the salesperson may give himself a reward, such as a walk or a treat. Afterwards, the salesperson completes the remaining ten phone contacts and rewards himself again. The results are 20 new phone contacts, which represent 33% more prospecting than before. It's all attitude and mind conditioning.

Instead of torturing yourself to get through the day, feed your mind constructive positive self-suggestions, such as saying, "With each and every contact I make, I'm getting better and better and closer to sales perfection; soon I'll be the best in what I do."

Positive mental images and positive statements create a positive environment and positive results.

The average person will accept living with his own negative thinking and use all kinds of excuses to blame others (a form of negative thinking) as to why he never had a chance to be successful.

The average person can make one failure a major setback. The person who thinks differently says, "I'm not going to stop! Each setback makes me stronger and more determined to succeed. And, if times get tougher, I'll be better prepared to succeed."

Positive self-suggestions have to be practiced every day. Write them down. Modify and refine them to your own personality, but never stop using them. Start out with only a few and then after a couple of months, add slowly to your list. The self-suggestion statements must be memorized and repeated daily.

These positive self-suggestions will change your life for the better. The average person will seldom or never use positive self-suggestions because that person does not believe he can improve or has no interest to improve. The person who believes in himself is the person who can change the world.

Living in New York City, I'm reminded often that many of the new immigrants to America have two driving forces. First, they want to do well because they want to share in America's wealth. Secondly, they want to bring their loved ones to America in order to share the wealth and enjoy what America offers. Do you see the mental conditioning?

Successful people have taught themselves to go beyond the average, ordinary lifestyle. They are not afraid to drive themselves hard and they never stop pursuing their goals to greatness.

I realize that not everyone can be the President of the United States or the wealthiest person on earth, just as not everyone can sing well. The important point is this: everyone can be better. That may mean working harder and it certainly means having better positive attitudes which result in your being better and greater than you are now. I would remind everyone, "Think it and it shall come to pass."

L.P. Jacks said, "The pessimist sees the difficulty in every opportunity; the optimist, the opportunity in every difficulty."

You can stop using defeatist words and statements. In order to improve, you should first write down the words and phrases you don't want to use again. Refuse to repeat these common self-defeating attitudes: "I can't"; "If I can"; "I'll try"; "I don't think I can"; "take it easy"; "I don't know if I can"; and "try to have a good day."

Replace the negative words, phrases, and attitudes. Reprogram your attitudes and words every day. By changing your words, which represent your thinking, you can change your life. Today someone will surely ask you, "How are you?" Avoid giving negative replies such as: "Oh, all right"; "Okay, I guess"; "as best as can be expected"; or "not bad."

Think before you answer. You are alive today, which means you are working to achieve something wonderful in your life. Let your answers be great answers: "I'm doing great!" "I'm feeling fantastic"; "I couldn't be feeling better." The positive answers will make you feel better and they feed your subconscious mind. How about: "It's great to be alive!"

You are warned not to eat too much junk food because it can hurt your body. So, too, you should not be filling your mind with junk attitudes and junk thoughts that prevent success. Be different by giving enthusiastic statements about how well you are coming along in your goals.

You can be different. You are smart enough to achieve greatness. You can set an example for the whole world to follow. You can make people glad that they met you. Lift everyone's spirits up. Make people look forward to seeing you again and again because they feel good around you. It may not be easy some days, but it is tremendously rewarding. And remember: If something great is to happen, then let it begin with you.

I've always loved making people feel better about themselves. It never hurts when we practice the admonition: "It's better to give than to receive." Helping others is good for your soul.

Abraham Lincoln said, "Nearly all men can stand adversity but if you want to test a man's character, give him power."

You have a lot more unused power than you have been using - the power to help others. Each one of us has been given this power. How can you apply this power today? Surprise others by helping them. I remember reading a sign in a dentist's office, "Ignore your teeth, they'll go away!"

If you ignore your power to help others and to help yourself, opportunities for greatness will wither away.

The Carinci Freedom Diet

Watching what you feed your mind is also true for your body. Imagine walking around all day with a twenty-pound weight strapped to your back. By the end of the day, you would feel exhausted, mentally drained, and would probably have a backache. Yet, many people are overweight. Many are considered obese. But, twenty pounds extra is not healthy. According to a 2002 Harris Poll, 80 percent of people older than 25 are overweight, based on the body mass index (BMI). Thirty-three percent of adults are 20 percent overweight. If you are overweight, imagine taking ten to twenty pounds off your body. How good would it feel to lose the weight? Extra weight is known to lead to diabetes, high blood pressure, bad knees, and back ailments. It makes sense to maintain your healthy weight. Remember: "To be all you can be, watch what you eat." Here is an easy-to-follow diet that you can use the rest of your life. The following diet should only be used by overweight people or by healthy people to maintain healthy weight, and always must be approved by your doctor.

<u>Monday to Friday</u>

Breakfast: 2 slices of toast or a muffin and fruit. or Bagel with very little cream cheese.

Lunch: Piece of fruit or salad and lite dressing, or mixed fruit cup.

Dinner: Anything you want: pasta, bread; hamburger. No dessert. (Total Freedom)

No alcoholic beverage allowed until the weekend.

After dinner snack:All the fruit you want (any kind), or carrot and celery sticks.

2-quarts of water before 10 P.M.

No other snacks allowed until the weekend.

<u>Friday, Saturday, and Sunday Evenings</u>

Dinner:Any choice of dinner allowed, including bread and pasta, within reason.

One dessert serving of any choice is allowed (Saturday and Sunday only).

One alcoholic beverage per weekend evening

is allowed.

2 quarts of water before 10 P.M.

<u>Saturday and Sunday:</u>

Lunch: Sandwich or salad, any fruit is O.K.

One serving of candy or chips during the
day or evening.

After 8:30 P.M., go back to weekday diet.

This is a simple way to diet without suffering too
much. Most diets can not be maintained for
long periods of time. This diet allows
"freedom" of choice at dinner. Therefore,
it can be maintained. Watch your weight loss
carefully. Do not overdo the diet and see
your doctor regularly for evaluations.

Good luck and good health.

*God grant me serenity to accept the
things I cannot change, courage to change
the things I can and wisdom to know the
difference. Living one day at a time,
enjoying one moment at a time.*

> *--St Francis of Assisi*
> *Founder of Franciscans*
> *(1182-1226)*

25
Death Can Be A Motivating Force

I've never met a person, I don't care what his condition, in whom I could not see possibilities. I don't care how much a man may consider himself a failure, I believe in him, for he can change the thing that is wrong in his life any time he is ready and prepared to do it. Whenever he develops the desire, he can take away from his life the thing that is defeating it. The capacity for reformation and change lies within.

--Rev. Dr. Preston Bradley

Renewed Efforts

The date is July 15th, 1999, a hot Saturday. The entire summer has been having record temperatures. Breaking news comes on the television, "John F. Kennedy Jr.'s small six passenger plane is missing."

As the day progresses, the news turns worse. The rescuers collect debris from the Piper Saratoga plane that Kennedy was piloting. Hope for survivors slowly turns grim, as John, his wife Caroline, and her sister are somewhere at bottom of the ocean near Martha's Vineyard.

John Kennedy, only 38, had a bright future ahead of him. He was successful in business and had purchased his own plane six months earlier. His mother, Jacqueline, had died only five years earlier from cancer at the age of 64. His father, President John F. Kennedy, was tragically assassinated at age 46.

As I watched the rescue turn into a recovery of the plane's wreckage, I was reminded how many young people are suddenly taken from us before they are able to live their lives out. The Kennedy family is certainly a family which has had to endure an unusual amount of loss and grief from the early deaths of their loved ones.

A little over a year earlier in 1998, Princess Diana had lost her life at age 36. We remember the great things she did in her short life and, yet, she had not quite found the peace and happiness in her personal life that she longed for. Her death brought about a widespread feeling of sadness that showed how much the world respected all she had done in her young life. She, too, could have done many more great things, if she had lived.

Many people look to God for some answer as to why young people die suddenly, while many people die in old age. We console ourselves by reasoning that God has a master plan. I, too, put my faith in God and believe that there is a divine master plan. But I have to admit my faith in God does not always give me answers about why death comes to the young. I believe I can only say as the psalmist said, "The Lord is my shepherd and I shall not want." (Psalm 23)

It may seem strange, but I draw an unusual amount of strength from the passing of a young person. Almost as if shocked by an electric current, I'm motivated into action. After the initial mourning, I look at the person's life and his accomplishments. Then I convince myself how lucky I am to have another day to live in order to accomplish something great. I don't want to ignore death; rather, I want to understand someone's death as a reminder that I have limited time to reach my goals.

When a young person dies, the awareness of the shortness of life comes rushing back at me. I stop procrastinating and work harder at getting out of any ruts I have created for myself. It's a wake up call. Many would try to convince me that I've done very well thus far in life, but I'm not satisfied and want to be remembered for accomplishing much more.

As I improve myself, I help others improve, who in turn, will help others to improve. This will eventually improve the world. The great thing about life is that anyone is capable of changing the world for the better. I am consumed with making a difference in this world.

Robert Kennedy said: "Few will have the greatness to bend history itself; but each of us can work to change a small portion of events, and in the total of all those acts will be written the history of this generation."

Napoleon Hill said, "Every adversity carries with it the seed of an equivalent benefit."

Carrying The Torch

Though a young person has died, that death can spur you on to renew your efforts to do something positive and great. Feeling disturbed by the knowledge of your own mortality is useful. You may be driven into positive action. It can be called "inspirational dissatisfaction." You must learn from everything you observe in your life. There's a lesson in everything. You only have to interpret it, learn from it, apply your inspiration, and make the most of your talent.

Are you ready for the hereafter? I'm certainly not! I have so much more to do, but I love the feeling of wanting to do so much more.

The hereafter is a long, long time. What accomplishments are you taking with you? What will you tell all the others in the hereafter about your great accomplishments? Did you leave the world a better place? Did you make a positive difference? It is never too late to attain your greatness. Yogi Berra said it best when he said, "It's not over till it's over."

Inspirational dissatisfaction, if used correctly, will motivate and drive you to take action. A successful life is a life of action, not of inaction. You are God's greatest miracle. You should be attaining great miracles with God's help in your life.

In my career field, I've gone from struggling to survive to doing extremely well. I realize that building a successful business is not easy and it doesn't appear to be getting any easier to keep a business growing. It's a real challenge. The challenge for me is to constantly change, to strive to improve, to continue to grow, to reinvent new ways of serving my clients, and, of course, never to be satisfied.

When I started out in insurance sales, my mind-set was not to fail. My fear of failing was a tremendous motivator at the start. All these years later, I find that failing is not a big concern because I have the tools to make it anywhere. My attitude, my knowledge, my belief in God, belief in mankind, and belief in myself are the qualities that help me, as an energized person, to succeed in almost anything.

My motivations, too, have changed over the years. What inspires me today never entered my mind more than 25 years ago. I really get fired up when I think about the associates that work with me. One of my burning desires now is to share my success as much as I possibly can, so that others can attain the success I have been able to achieve. The drive to encourage others, to help others to become successful and earn higher incomes, is what keeps me committed to improving and further advancing my sales agency. After all these years in my field, I am still energized and passionate about selling insurance and my commitment to helping people protect their families.

You need that inner force, something special inside that makes you work harder, longer and smarter than the average person.

One constant burning desire that keeps driving me forward, is to grab hold of the torch that others, who have passed on, carried. In my mind I visualize that I've been given the responsibility to achieve the things others did not have the chance to finish.

It is a great honor carrying the torch for them, celebrating their remembrance. I picture them watching and cheering me on. I truly believe that each and every person we think about in the hereafter can, in turn, think and visualize us here. Maybe it is my own little fantasy. Maybe I am all wrong. But you can find your own burning desire, something that drives you on to greatness.

George Burns, the comedian, is a good example of someone who kept entertaining people until the day he died. Entertaining others was his life. He taught all of us that you do not stop achieving because society expects you to at a certain age. As he got older, we kept rooting for him while he kept achieving new accomplishments in films and stage work.

George Burns has inspired me to keep dreaming of new goals. I have an obligation to those who are looking down, watching me, those who are rooting for me.

What do you want to achieve? What new goals should you be accomplishing? Just picture all those whom you have known who have passed on. Picture them supporting, watching, and rooting for you. You really do have your own fan club.

Imagine, dream, achieve, and become.

I plan to win even when common sense should tell me that I no longer have a chance. Even when I have been playing at my worst, or when all the breaks have been going against me, I approach each new day, each new hole, as a glorious opportunity to get going again.

--Arnold Palmer
Golfer/Four times Masters Winner

26
I Must Be More Now

The people who get on in this world
are the people who get up and look
for the circumstances they want, and
if they can't find them, make them.

--George Bernard Shaw
English Dramatist
(1856-1950)

One Day Never Forgotten

On September 11,[th] 2001, I remember being in my hotel room at the Taj Mahal Hotel in Atlantic City. I stood shaving at the bathroom mirror at 8:55 A.M. when my wife called out to me to come see the television news. The World Trade Center had been hit by a plane at 8:45 A.M. I quickly finished my shaving and sat on the edge of the bed staring at the television screen. While a great, dark cloud of smoke billowed out of the tall building, I tried to understand how a pilot could possibly hit such a huge structure.

At 9:03 A.M., I saw the second plane in a precise angle purposely crash and disappear into the South Tower. I yelled for my wife, who was then taking her turn in the bathroom, to see what had happened. We heard about two more plane crashes that day: the Pentagon was hit at 9:43 A.M. and the downing of the passenger jet in Somerset County, PA, took place at 10:10 A.M.

I had witnessed a tragic, historical event that changed America and the world. The security and safety Americans had taken for granted disappeared in the fireballs of four planes that crashed in New York City, Pennsylvania, and Washington, D.C.

I was thankful that I had no relatives who were lost in the World Trade Center attacks. Yet, I felt that a part of me died that day. My belief in mankind was shaken.

In the following days and weeks, New Yorkers and Americans experienced pain that seemed endless as the country witnessed the devastation of the attacks. Rescuers worked day after day in a painstaking search for all the victims.

The craziness of the world's brutality had finally reached our streets and lives. How could it happen? Terrorism was never supposed to be this close to our homes. Bombs and terrorist acts had always been things that happened in far away places. I had only heard about violence in some other country, some other place, but I was not prepared to witness almost three thousand people dying in New York City.

How do you keep from having this horrific attack drain your energy and affect your emotions? How can you keep motivated to achieve positive action? How can you forge ahead? It is hard not to dwell on the uncertainty of future terrorist acts against Americans. How can we not be consumed with worry and doubt?

You must first put your faith and trust in God, believing that good prevails over evil. You have to have faith in the government, the president, our elected officials, and our proven democracy. The 9/11 attack on our buildings and cities was the warning bell alerting us to protect our democracy from those who hate democratic principles and ideals.

9/11 does not have to drive us to hate. If others hate America and perceive it as being too selfish, then this is the time for Americans to help other people in other countries in new ways. America needs to be that special light in the world that shows others that democracy is always a better choice, rather than terrorism, hatred, and all forms of tyranny.

9/11 is a reminder that we should live to do more each day because each day is a blessing not be taken lightly. Being alive means you have been given more time to accomplish more good things in your life. Your life multiplied by time equals greater accomplishments.

Remember the Parable of the Talents and the son that hid his talents so not to risk losing them? Meanwhile, his other brother multiplied his talents by using them. The lesson is that you have talents that should be used. I believe many people never use their talents to their fullest extent. That means that there are billions of people in the world who are living lives below their potential. The great tragedy

273

is that many don't care. They get up, do some work, and go to sleep having done the minimum.

Imagine how much better the world would be if some of those billions of people started working to attain new goals for themselves and were driven to achieve greatness. The whole world would improve as billions of people start to excel, discover new inventions, and make the entire A better place.

By using your talents and developing new skills, not only do you reap greatness, you can change the world and make it a better place.

There comes a time in a man's life when to get where he has to go-if there are no doors or windows-he walks through a wall.

--Bernard Malamud
American Author
(1914-1986)

I believe that the victims of 9/11 and all of our friends and relatives who have passed on are looking down on you and me.

I believe in God and in the hereafter. I truly believe there is much more than this here-and-now, our flesh and bones, and our time we are given on earth. I believe our time on earth is a test, and we get a score as to how well we have used our talents.

9/11 taught the whole nation about getting through grief and moving forward with a new determination to stand strong for freedom, democracy, and the noble goals of America. Americans had a choice -- to give in to the many heartless and cold-blooded killers holed up throughout the world, or to take freedom, democracy, and the good things about America to other parts of the world.

You have choices in your life, too. You can be a follower or you can lead others with your creative imagination and example. You can be average or you can "be different" by attaining greater goals. You can be mediocre or you can attain greatness. I choose to be different in order to achieve greatness.

Man's happiness in life is the result of
man's own effort and is neither the gift
of God nor a spontaneous natural product.

--Ch'en Tu-hsiu
Chinese Editor
(1879-1942)

You are like the tree that is destined to grow tall, the bird that soars high, and the water that flows with new life to quench the thirst of others.

Your very birth was a fabulous miracle. You have the talents to do the extraordinary. By using your creative imagination, your life will become an outpouring of miracles that will help others.

Your opportunities abound. May you soar to greatness every day.

*He has achieved success who has lived
well, laughed often and loved much; who
has gained the respect of intelligent
men and the love of little children; who
has filled his niche and accomplished his
task; who has left the world better than
he found it, whether by an improved poppy,
a perfect poem, or a rescued soul; who has
never lacked appreciation of earth's beauty
or failed to express it; who has always
looked for the best in others and given
them the best he had; whose life was an
inspiration; whose memory a benediction.*

--Bessie Stanley
18th Century Poet

Self-Suggestion Statements

Today I begin my new life. The old life of mediocrity, compromise, and weariness has been laid to rest. Today I am born anew, with all the enthusiasm of a child. For as a child, I was going to conquer the world. Today I will replace the old with the new, and the new will slowly become habit through daily repetition.

With the new Power Ideas that I have learned, I will be successful. For now on, I know why many fail and I will avoid that road filled with pits of failure. Never again will I feel pity for myself, for now I realize I have all I need to change my life for the better. I understand now that I have so much more than many others who have debilitating impairments, who achieve greatness many times despite severe obstacles.

Never again will I follow the followers in life. For now I know that I can lead the way. And even though I may take wrong turns, never again will I be deterred. I now know so much more. Even Thomas Edison had more than 10,000 mistakes before achieving his great invention of the light bulb. Failure will never again intimidate or depress me, rather it will be my steppingstone to victory. For now, I understand that victory is always near the end of the journey, not within the first few steps. I will push on. I will rise to the occasion. Each new day will be the best day of my life, and the world will take notice and admire this new attitude.

From this day forward, I will be sure to spread this new positive attitude in all I do and for all others to see, feel, and sense. I know it is far better to wear a protective armor made out of motivation and a positive disposition, which will repel all negativity. And in return, I will allow the subconscious, the more powerful part of my brain to absorb and retain only positive motivating thoughts, which it will send back out like the beacon of a lighthouse. The bible says: "Ask and it shall be given. Seek and you shall find. Knock and the door shall open. For the one who asks will always receive."

Are we not what we eat? And do we not become and achieve what we think? Never again will I allow others to sense negativity from me. The world is full of pessimistic individuals, preaching doom and gloom. I choose a better way to live. There are so many others, departed and living, who have believed in me as someone special. Do I not owe it to them, myself and my creator to accomplish greatness? For my enthusiasm and charisma will spur positive actions and responses from others. I now know that a positive attitude is contagious. I will forever lift the attitudes of all that I meet, knowing full well that when I help another - I help myself.

Always, and from this day on – I will love all people whom I meet each day, no matter how they treat or react to me. How can I love myself without loving all others first? For now I am aware that I am the greatest living miracle that my newborn mind was first exposed to. I know now that my odds at being born and winding up with my exact personality were millions to one. So, I will love all of God's other miracles as I love myself. Always, will I show my love to others, looking for the good, the gold inside of everyone. Because I now know every human being has good inside of him, though, sometimes, hidden. I also know that showing my love first will bring forth love out of others. Just as an animal studies a human's eyes, looking for danger, friend or foe, all whom I have eye contact with will study me for love, hatred, despair, sadness or fear. I will project only love.

Now that I possess these Power Ideas, I will motivate myself each day onward to success. Never again will I allow others to keep me down. I will arise each morning with renewed energy and confidence, eager to unwrap that special gift of a new day. I will push on harder when others give up. And I will move to the top like heavy cream, rich in texture, with my convictions. I vow to always consume positive uplifting thoughts, but if I should wander, as I may, I will quickly get back on track. Do we not watch what our bodies consume? Is it not paramount to feed our minds, which controls our bodies – only the purest, most uplifting, enthusiastic thoughts?

Now I realize that like the bodybuilder developing his body, I must maintain my greatest asset - my mind. And I now vow to feed that mind inspiration and motivation, through books, tapes, and actions. My mind must stay in shape like the muscles of the bodybuilder. And I also realize that I am different from others. But I will never act as though I am better than another. For no one is ever better than anyone else, just different – through attitudes, personality, inspiration, thoughts, and enthusiasm. I will be successful; it's inevitable, because my aggressiveness will create opportunities for my success.

Suggested Reading

The following are related books quoted from, or those which may bring additional light on strategies listed in this book.

Insight: monthly publication by Nightingale-Conant Corp., 2004.

You Can If You Think You Can!: by Norman Vincent Peale, Fireside, 1987.

Long Time No See: by Dr. No-Yong Park, Exposition Press

Success Through A Positive Mental Attitude: By Napoleon Hill and W. Clement Stone, Pocket Books, 1991.

The Greatest Salesman In The World: by Og Mandino, Bantam Books, 1983.

The Choice: by Og Mandino, Bantam Books, 1990.

The Power Of Your Subconscious Mind: by Dr. Joseph Murphy, Bantam Books, 2001.

The Magic Of Thinking Big: by David Schwartz, Fireside, 1987.

The Magic Of Believing: by Claude M. Bristol, Pocket Books, 1991.

David St. Clair's Lessons in Instant ESP: By David St. Clair, Signet, 1986.

Beyond Survival: by Gerald Coffee, Putnam Publishing Group, 1990.

The Conquest Of Happiness: by Bertrand Russell, Liveright Publishing, 1996.

The One Minute Manager: by Kenneth Blanchard & Spencer Johnson, Berkley Books, 1983.

In Search Of Excellence: by Tom Peters, Warner Books, 1988.

Heart Of A Champion: by Bob Richards, Books-on-Demand, 2004

21st Century Positioning: by Jack & Garry Kinder, Taylor Publishing, 1999

Don't Sweat The Small Stuff...and it's all small stuff: by Richard Carlson, Ph.D., Hyperion, 1997.

About The Author

John Paul Carinci has been a successful business owner for 30 years. Currently, he is President of Carinci Insurance Agency Inc., with over 200 brokers. John, is also an author, songwriter, and poet. He is the CEO of Better Off **Dead Productions Inc., a movie production company.**

As a writer, some of John's other works **include; "Better Off Dead," "A Second Chance", "In Exchange Of Life", "Better Off Dead Again", and "Reflections In Poetry."**

John, is also co-writer of the screenplays: "Better Off Dead," and "A Second Chance," which was adapted from his novels, and may be produced as motion pictures in the coming months.